THE ROAR OF HER STORY

HILARY SALZMAN

THE ROAR OF HER STORY

How to tell everyday stories to
attract your dream clients and build a
business that's unapologetically you.

THE UNBOUND PRESS

Cover art: Ellie Bowie

ISBN 978-1-916529-22-9 Paperback
ISBN 978-1-916529-23-6 Ebook

The Unbound Press
www.theunboundpress.com

HILARY SALZMAN

THE ROAR OF HER STORY

How to tell everyday stories to
attract your dream clients and build a
business that's unapologetically you.

THE UNBOUND PRESS

Cover art: Ellie Bowie

ISBN 978-1-916529-22-9 Paperback
ISBN 978-1-916529-23-6 Ebook

The Unbound Press
www.theunboundpress.com

Hey unbound one!

Welcome to this magical book brought to you by The
Unbound Press.

At The Unbound Press we believe that when women
write freely from the fullest expression of who they are, it
can't help but activate a feeling of deep connection and
transformation in others. When we come together, we
become more and we're changing the world, one book at
a time!

This book has been carefully crafted by both the
contributors and publisher with the intention of inspiring
you to move ever more deeply into who you truly are.

We hope that this book helps you to connect with your
Unbound Self and that you feel called to pass it on to
others who want to live a more fully expressed life.

With much love,
Nicola Humber

Founder of The Unbound Press

www.theunboundpress.com

To the voices that refuse to be silenced
and the stories that demand to be told.

To my daughter Esme for inspiring me
that we can and must do better.

This book is for you.
May you all find the strength to roar.

CONTENTS

AUTHOR'S NOTE

Hello and welcome to *The Roar of Her Story.*

In a world so full of choice, that makes your head spin and your eyes rattle, thank you for picking this book.

Before we get too deep into the juicy details, there are a few things I need to ask you to do.

Firstly, try and put aside all pre-conceived ideas of what storytelling is. That includes thinking storytelling is yet another new fad to get you to invest more time and money learning something you'll never actually get round to using (it isn't – and you will – because you're likely doing it already) or any of the following myths:

1. Storytelling can only be used when being really creative or 'fun.' It's not for proper business marketing or serious issues.

Codswallop. Storytelling is a way to get your message not only heard but embedded in the hearts and minds of your audience. If you're seeking proof, just look at the way charities such as MIND and Crisis use stories to raise awareness.

2. A story must start with 'Once upon a time' and end with 'and then they lived happily ever after.'

Not all stories are fairy tales. Stories are a great way to start serious conversations and can humanise subjects that are otherwise hard to talk about. *Humans of New York* by Brandon Stanton is an incredible example of this. (Google it and thank me later).

3. Storytelling can only be used for nice 'lifestyle-type' products.

Wrong. One of my go-to examples of human storytelling is a shipping container business called Maersk. You couldn't get any less 'lifestyle' if you tried.

4. You can only be a good storyteller if you're a great writer.

Poppycock. Storytelling trumps beautiful writing every time. You really have no excuse.

Secondly, if there's a nagging voice inside your head that's been holding you back from storytelling in the past, I want you to sit down and have a stern word with it.

This book is not going to make your inner critic disappear, but you'll likely find it pretty handy for batting it away when it gets too close for comfort, just like a pesky wasp.

Not sure what this voice might sound like? Here are a few things it's likely to be telling you:

"Your business is too small, too new, too uneventful for storytelling to make any difference."

"You hated English at school, so why are you even pretending you could be a storyteller?"

"Nobody is going to be interested in what you have to say or where you've been; they just want to buy from you and get the hell outta Dodge."

And my personal favourite, "You haven't got a story to tell. You're too boring."

So now I've got all that out in the open, how about a few more truths?

This book is not your bog-standard self-help guide that promises all the answers if only you do exactly what I tell you to. Far from it. This book is about arming you with the knowledge, and more importantly, the confidence, to understand and believe in the power of your voice and how you can turn your experiences and perspectives into stories to attract your dream clients and fulfil your purpose, creating meaningful connections whilst building a business that reflects your brilliantly original and totally unapologetic self.

I want this book to be something practical you can use immediately – folding down the corners of pages that excite you, highlighting paragraphs you don't want to forget, scribbling notes and testing out ideas as you go.

And I want it to be something you come back to – like an old-friend – when you need a bit of encouragement or inspiration. I didn't put my heart and soul into this book for it to sit on your shelf and gather dust and dead woodlice. You've been told.

If you're ready to open the lid on all your inner thoughts and desires, discover the voice that's been waiting (slightly impatiently) inside and turn your stories into kick ass marketing tools that are THE BEST WAY to get the shit done you really want to – including building trusted communities of customers, followers and collaborators who love the hell out of what you do and sell and aren't afraid to tell everyone they meet about you and your business – then what are you waiting for?

INTRODUCTION

*"Owning our story and loving ourselves through
the process is the bravest thing we'll ever do."*

Brené Brown

Back in 2019, I consciously uncoupled from the marketing agency I co-owned. In all honesty, things hadn't been working for some time. We were sleeping in separate beds. The passion had gone. There was no major upset – no-one had had an affair. Things simply fizzled out. "It's not you, it's me."

As hard as it was to walk away from a business I had played a key role in building and a team I had helped grow (and that was making me a lot more money than I earn now), when it came down to it, it was a simple decision. I didn't fit. Scrap that, that's negative talk. What the business had become no longer fitted with me – who I was, what I wanted from life…more importantly what I believed. It was time to take charge and follow my heart once and for all.

Yes, it was bloody scary when it finally sunk in that the responsibility of winning business and getting paid sat entirely with me and me alone. But you know what? Despite feeling anxious, I didn't care. And why not? Because the feeling that I finally owned my story kicked my fears right out of the park. I was free. More importantly, I was **me**.

How much of this is sounding familiar to you?

Maybe you've struggled to know where you fitted and what you wanted to do professionally? Pretended to be someone you're not. Overlooked things you knew directly conflicted with your own values, just to try and fit in. Compromised job fulfilment and creativity for profits. Perhaps, through knock-backs, you've opted to keep in the shadows, head down, not making a fuss, despite not doing what your heart tells you that you should be. Or maybe you've felt frustrated, under-appreciated, desperate to share your wisdom, your experience, your incredible, beautiful view of the world but unable to find the voice to do so.

Whether you're new in the business world or part of the furniture, if you have ever at any time felt afraid or unsure about using your voice and telling your story, this book is for you. In fact it's for anyone who has ever feared judgement, felt afraid or changed their narrative to suit others or their perceived expectations. Anyone who has had their voice silenced by others or by their own devious inner critic, or haven't felt they deserve to take up a space. Anyone with a story to tell. And that, by the way, is everyone.

Back to my story for a mo. I've always been a dreamer. As a child I planned a life doing jobs I had absolutely no talent for; a fashion designer, a photographer, a radio presenter. I even went through a stage believing I could be an actor, dragging my poor mum from our home in Oxfordshire to North London to audition for the National Youth Theatre. Slight problem – I was talentless. Couldn't act, couldn't sing and had never as much as stepped onto a stage.

I was so desperate to be 'someone,' that I ignored the one talent and true love that was staring me firmly in my NHS spectacled face: writing. Maybe it was because writing felt like breathing to me. A natural, unconscious act that kept me alive. Feeling lost at sea with who I was, who I wanted to be, who others expected me to be. I would take myself away to imaginary worlds – little stories written in books I would crudely illustrate and hold together with staples, poems, pretend newspaper articles, radio show scripts that I would perform to no-one. It felt so natural to write, that it wasn't until I was 16 that I realised I could make a career from it.

So I studied hard, applied to study journalism at university and got a place on a prestigious BA in Journalism course at London's City University. I hated it. Not the journalism, but that was only two hours a week. Uni life wasn't for me. Not for the first time in my life, I felt like an outsider. Everyone else seemed so much more mature than me, experienced, focussed, driven, better writers, destined for success where I was not. I'm was convinced I got my place through pity. Surely there were better writers who deserved to be on the course more than me? Or maybe they were desperate to fill places that year. Whatever the reason, I never once believed it was because I had a real shot at being a journalist.

So I quit.

Less than a year in.

And went to work for a local newspaper that, too, was a disaster. Under the alleged tutorage of my editor – a sweaty, beady-eyed man who used to work for the tabloids (red flag, hello?!) – I was thrown in at the proverbial deep end. His idea of mentoring me mainly involved shouting at me for all the things I didn't yet know (that I thought I was there to learn). A few weeks in, I discovered I was the sixth trainee reporter to go through the newsroom in two years. All but one of my predecessors were women.

"If you can't cut it here, you'll never work anywhere," I remember my editor growling at me after a, quite frankly traumatic, telephone interview with the 80s pop star Marc Almond. And I walked. And I honestly believed that I would never write again.

I felt a failure. No degree. Living at home without a clue what I was going to do next, I got a job in a call centre. It was the pits. I had to listen to people report stains on their furniture or carpet and negotiate the often-embarrassing truth out of them so I could recommend the next course of action. "Come on, Mr Brown. We all know that strange white mark that just 'appeared' isn't mayonnaise!" Weirdly, as bizarre a job as this was, it taught me a lot about myself, namely that I really liked working in a team and that I was good with people.

There I was. Still yearning to write but hating the isolation of journalism. Loving being in a team but knowing a life-long career in insurance claims wasn't going to be the one for me. So where else do you head? You've got it – marketing. Communications, people, problem solving and WRITING. My first 'proper' job was a marketing assistant for an-up-and-coming IT security company. Oh, the glamour, the glitz, the massive £13,000 salary – I was on cloud nine. Until reality, once again, kicked in – a depressingly common consequence of being born with two XX chromosomes rather than an XY.

As my friends were chugging pints and pulling all-nighters to get their dissertations done, I was politely declining advances from drunken male IT reps at the conferences I organised and laughing off the belittling jokes about me being in the 'colouring in' department (and that was from the CEO!) I loved my job, for a while anyway, but something very soon became clear. I was too young to have an opinion. And then I was too female. If I ever mustered up the courage to speak up in a meeting, I hated the way my chest would turn a bright red mottled colour, like the rancid corned beef we used to get at primary school. Hot sweats, clammy hands. All eyes on me. "Speak up." I'd start to make my point, excitement, passion even, festering inside me, but the words wouldn't come. My voice would crack. Honestly believing I was about to cry, I'd retreat, sit back down, only to have someone else make the very same point I was about to, and be applauded in the room for it. Lost opportunities, stolen ideas, this went on for years. Until I started to find my feet.

I soon realised I had strong opinions and, when I was able to articulate them, people were starting to listen. I had a natural aptitude for marketing; I just got it and the results spoke for themselves. Rung by rung, I started the slow tiresome trek up the ladder. I got promoted, changed companies, got a pay rise, managed staff.

And then, one day, one of those staff said something which changed it all. "You're a bully." You what? I remember even the HR manager (let's call him Rob because, well, that was his name), who was hosting the team building session gasp with surprise. The bottom of my stomach felt like it had fallen out, a gooey horrid mess on the floor.

"Can you qualify what you mean by that?" Rob said.

"Sure, Hilary is a bully. Just look at the way she pushed that <insert some boring corporate initiative here that I surely can't remember the details of> through, didn't give us a chance to have our say, didn't want to hear it." I was mortified. This didn't sound like me at all. Of course, I immediately apologised (that's the people pleaser in me) and got ready for a session of mental torture and self-flagellation. But then I stopped to think about it. I hadn't pushed it through. I had consulted the team, sought opinions, worked through ideas, rejected plenty … Oh, light bulb moment alert. This person did bring me an idea. My experience told me it wouldn't work, so I explored it with them and presented a considered case why we wouldn't be progressing with it. I had an opinion. I backed it up with sound evidence. I asserted the responsibility I had to my team and the business. But yes, I was the bully.

So I retreated once again. Head down, did my job (but nothing more to draw attention to myself), cried more than once in the staff toilets and dreamt about a day when I didn't feel useless or alone. I hated the office politics, the brown nosing, the backstabbing. I just wanted to make people happy but no-one ever seemed to be.

And then I got pregnant.

Overjoyed, I felt like I had purpose once again. Work could wait – I was going to be a mum.

But do you know the one thing no-one ever tells you about being a mum? It's that, once you are, everyone else seems to pretty much forget you were ever anything else. Once again, I struggled to fit in, this time with my post-natal groups. I actively swerved as many 'mummy and baby activities' as possible and yearned for a conversation that didn't start with, "How's your little one sleeping?" Ahhh for fuck's sake. I have a brain. I have intelligent thoughts. Why not ask me about those? But apparently, no-one ever does. And that sucks.

Twelve months later, I headed back to the office. Excited that, surely in a corporate environment, my voice would matter for something more than breast pump recommendations.

I didn't keep a diary at the time, but if I did it would have read something a little like this:

Day 1.

Back at HQ and realised that despite my years' absence, nothing whatsoever has changed. Projects I left are still ongoing. Lots of people came to say, 'Hi' and ask me how my baby was, even though they didn't care. No-one asked me how I was.

Had 3 meetings about meetings about meetings and told 57,000 people that no, I couldn't attend the next one on Thursday as I only work Monday – Wednesday. Cue eye rolls and huffs.

Day 2.

Nursery called at 11am. My daughter has a temperature. Took the rest of the day off.

Day 3.

Poked my eyes out with sticks. Plotted my escape.

Okay. Let's summarise. Aged 29, I had never felt I'd fitted anywhere. When I did find a job I liked, I was made to, 1, feel my voice didn't matter and, 2, feel really bad about myself. Becoming a parent, although wonderful, confused matters even more (who even am I now??). To make things worse, by this stage, I had also got divorced. From a man that was so loud and outgoing that, over the years, I had shrunk – not grown and become more than accustomed to letting someone else speak for me. Frustratingly, this whole experience added credence to the already very loud, very annoying voice in my head telling me, "YOU ARE NOTHING." Say hello to a major mental health blip, some terrible relationships, and a small matter of STARTING MY OWN BUSINESS.

I know my story is not unique. And I absolutely acknowledge my privilege – yes it was hard for me personally, but I'm a white middle class woman, meaning my life is fundamentally easier than others. But none of this makes how it made me feel any less real. And, likewise, for you too.

If you're a child of the late 1970s or 80s like me, you may well have grown up with at least one parent telling you, "There are children starving in Africa" when you refused to finish your Birds Eye potato waffles and baked beans. My mum still uses some form of this narrative now. And I get it. It can be seen as encouraging to remind you that your problems are no way near as bad as others but – and it's a massive but – being made to feel like your problems don't matter because of this, well, that's an altogether different kettle of fish. Yet this is how so many of us in our 30s, 40s, 50s and 60s have grown up thinking.

We shouldn't complain, shouldn't stand up when we see something that's wrong; we should toe the line, stick to the status quo, not make a fuss. And so, when we truly believe in something, when we see something we really want to go for, knowing deep down not only will it make us feel fulfilled but will help others too, we're compelled to downplay it all. "I like your business." "Oh this old thing…" We don't believe we have a right to carve out a space to be seen, heard, listened to, admired. We just need to keep quiet, keep our heads down … but not anymore.

Society is changing (thank fuck) – maybe not as fast as we would all like, but it's happening. And we, as female business owners, as thought leaders, as downright kick ass women, can make a serious difference.

So why does all this matter?

My voice matters to me because there have been too many times when other people have made me think it matters less. The times when I mustered up the courage to speak out, I felt guilty for taking up space, embarrassed for getting emotional, and often too scared to do it again. I've changed my voice to suit the agendas and desires of others (again, that's the people pleaser in me). I've said things I don't believe in to fit into a mould that makes me feel uncomfortable to my core, simply because I was too scared to speak my mind, trapped in a spiral of the "I'm not good enough" chatter running through my mind: "Women are less capable than men," "Be seen and not heard," (providing you look pretty), "Don't upset the apple cart," "Know your place."

Your voice matters to me because I don't want anyone else feeling this way. And because I believe in the power of a shared, collective voice to make real change happen. And that change starts right here, right now. You and me.

The Roar of Her Story is a new mantra, celebrating the power of the female voice and creating a space where all underrepresented voices are welcomed, calling on shared experiences and learnings, to protect the stories that are so important to us and create new narratives to replace those that no longer fit the world we want. And in doing this, sending a message that we're here to be heard. Yes, we might struggle from time to time (thanks, society, for all the added pressure you load on women). No, we don't always get it right. But if real change is to happen, if we're to progress collectively and individually to achieve the things we deserve, whether that's growing a business, landing the dream job, supporting a cause you believe in or just getting the people you care about to understand you that little bit better, our voices really do bloody matter. And it's time we all did something about it.

Don't believe me that your voice and your stories can do all that? All sounds a bit woo woo?

I bet you by the end of this book, you won't just believe it, you'll be living it. And your stories will be making a difference – whether to one, 100, or 10,000 people.

SETTING YOUR STORY STRATEGY

How to take what you're going to learn and feed it into your business

Let's assume you've finished this book. You're feeling more confident about your voice and have a better understanding of the value your story holds in connecting with your dream clients. What happens next?

You get out there and tell it, of course! In fact, incorporating storytelling into your sales, marketing and content plans will really help you attract and retain customers, build more profitable long lasting relationships and achieve your ambitions around growth, success and balance.

In a nutshell (and we will cover this is more detail over the coming chapters), stories in business serve three essential purposes; to grab attention, to build trust and to create advocacy ie getting those that buy from you to tell others how great you are.

Rather cunningly, this aligns exactly with how people buy.

Your business goal: Increase brand awareness

Your dream client's response: "I see you."

Story strategy: Use lots of stories to grab attention and raise awareness of your brand.

Speak directly to your customers' problems to show you understand them, but don't focus too much on specific products or services at this stage.

Your business goal: Build trust

Your dream client's response: "I believe in what you have to say – and I want to be part of it."

Story strategy: Use your stories to build trust, position yourself as an expert and show your willingness to help others.

Sharing your personal values here and insights into you as a person (good and bad) really helps create connections. Authenticity and honesty are key.

Your business goal: Create advocacy

Your dream client's response: "I love what you do/sell and I want to tell others about you."

Story strategy: Success stories reassure your customers they're making (or have already made) the right choice.

Why not give your customers a platform for sharing their stories about you? Ask them for a testimonial and re-share anything they say about you. It's ready-made content, perfect for the job!

SOMETHING TO THINK ABOUT:

Before you delve too much into this book,
consider what you want your stories to do for you.
What purpose will they serve, and how will this
support your growth strategy or marketing and
content plans?

MY PROMISE TO YOU

Over the coming chapters, you'll uncover all the different elements you need to create a story-led strategy for your business, including my template approach, which you can personalise for every story you create.

Don't worry if you're short on ideas of stories you can tell – I'll be sharing plenty of ideas and inspiration to help you find the stories your audience really wants – and needs you to tell.

By the time you turn the final page, you will be able to:

Craft epic narratives using your brand's one-of-a-kind voice: Be clear on your brand story: purpose, vision, mission and values. Understand your dream clients – their needs, their values, their shared experiences. Be able to explore the different business stories that you can tell to support your brand story and connect with your audience.

Open up to your audience: Understand why vulnerability is the new strength in storytelling. Be able to explore your vulnerable side and know how this can give you power when it comes to building meaningful and trusted relationships to grow your business and achieve your dreams.

Build expert-level stories: Structure stories that captivate your audience, evoke emotion and leave a lasting impact. Weave together plot, character, dialogue and theme to create a cohesive and compelling story that keeps people hooked from start to finish.

Nurture emotional connections: Paint vivid pictures with your words to appeal to your audience's senses and trigger emotional responses in their brains to inform decision making and encourage them to take action and buy from you.

Engage your audience with story-led content: Seek out powerful stories within your business and use them to build trust and credibility with your audience. Create multiple purpose story-led content to adapt across all your marketing channels including social media, your website and in person marketing. Find the way that best suits your style and resonates with your audience.

Create a storytelling community: Build a community for sharing stories and experiences with your dream clients to support your purpose and further the social causes you support. Use your story to address and overcome the things you see as wrong in the world.

Reflect and reimagine: Understand how to pay attention to your audience's needs and seek feedback. Have the tools to continuously refine your storytelling skills, learn from other storytellers and consistently practise and refine your craft. Unveil your storytelling legacy.

ROAR! Learn what it means to roar with your story and unveil your storytelling legacy.

A FINAL NOTE: BE WARY OF UNHELPFUL STORIES

I would love to find anyone who has never told themselves a story that's limited their ability to do something – or sent them into a spiral of doom and catastrophe. We all do it. It's part of being human. And for a big part – we're quickly proven wrong, and the story simply disappears.

But what happens when a story we tell ourselves doesn't go away? When actually, the voice in our head telling it over and over again, seems to be getting so loud we're not sure it will ever stop?

Your inner critic, the naughty chimp, whatever you call it, the unhelpful stories we tell ourselves are a real thing. For women especially, they can really get in the way of us achieving what we're truly capable of, especially when they reinforce self-limiting beliefs and societal expectations.

I want to introduce you to Dr Katie Morris. Before I tell you anything about her, take a read of an excerpt from her personal brand story that I worked on with her:

A Rebel with a Cause

Nurtured by my parents to be whatever I wanted and inspired by my Mum's journey from 14-year-old school leaver to university professor, it never crossed my mind that being a woman would ever hold me back (despite the inequalities that, on reflection, were present all around). At school, I developed a love of literature and from this, grew an understanding of the complexities of people's lives and their struggles. I always stood up for what I believed in and was never afraid to challenge authority when I felt something was unjust or unfair. As I began work in the NHS as a clinical psychologist, I channelled my belief in doing what's right to make a real difference in people's lives and also to challenge the things I saw around me that weren't working.

Frustrated by a medical model so out of kilter with everything I had studied and experienced in mental health, I felt compelled to leave the NHS to seek a structure I knew was right – for clients and those treating them. I didn't want to set up alone, and I was desperate to create something bigger than me, grounded in values that would provide flexibility as my young family grew.

Empowering a Better Future

Skip forward five years, and I've built a business I'm genuinely proud of, providing a proven model for clients requiring psychological services structured around their needs and strong clinical governance.

A new way of providing services. And a new way of working for psychologists. Free from the NHS's constraints and acting in the interest of what I believe to be ethically correct.

What do you take from that story? Maybe that Katie sounds like a kick ass woman unafraid to get not just what she wants from life but is committed to helping others get what they need. Perhaps you're inspired, wanting to have the same fearless approach in your life? After all, this was someone that had been labelled an 'anarchist' and 'rule-breaker' at school. So would you be surprised if I told you the reason Katie and I connected in the first place was because the fear of opening up to her audience was holding her back?

Since setting up her first private psychology clinic, The Purple House Clinic, Katie had felt a change deep within her, a new found drive, passion for business, a clear sense of direction. No less committed to the psychology profession, Katie realised these strengths that had always existed within her but had never been given the air to breath, could help her make an even bigger impact on her vision to build a force for good.

The Purple House Clinic became a space for other psychologists who had experienced the same as Katie within the NHS and needed a supportive, less risky route to continue their practice privately as well as build their own business.

But something played on Katie's mind. To really make a success of this growing franchise, she needed to commit 100% to the business. That meant giving up seeing clients directly herself. And that's where the problem crept in. She struggled with the decision – deep in her bones she wanted to do it and knew it was the right way forward – but rather that she feared a loss in an important part of her identity. She's spent nearly two decades helping clients change their lives. How could she let this work go? And what would her franchisees make of her choice? Would it take away her credibility?

Of course these are all valid questions, but sadly for so many of us, they become solid walls that stop us from ever pursuing the things we really want, no matter how happy we know they could make us feel. Katie was prepared to let that happen but it didn't make it any easier for her.

So together we worked through her story. We looked at how we could tell a combined tale that continued to highlight her expertise but showed how the progression of her mission meant that by focussing on the business, she could help even more people – psychologists and clients alike.

If I'm to be truthful, there was also a big element of taking a leap of faith, believing me (and others around her) that everything would be OK. And it was. As of 2024, The Purple House Clinic has 7 franchisees and 11 clinics around the UK, a number that continues to grow as more people buy into Katie's story.

And did she find that people respected her less for making a move away from working with clients to full time management of Purple House? Nobody even mentioned it. Funny that isn't it?! Rather, she got to build new parts to her identity and throw herself full on into growing her business and making it a success. This was always going to be far more rewarding than splitting herself in half.

So how do we stand up to those naughty voices in our head? Like I recommended to Katie, I like to start by squaring up to them. It might help for you to write down all those stories you tell yourself that could be holding you back – "I'm not good enough, "Last time I tried something new, I failed," "If I get this wrong, I'll just be proving everyone right," etc, etc. Then you need to call them out.

SOMETHING TO DO:

One by one, write down what the actual reality is. If you struggle with this, try and find evidence that backs up your negative stories. For example, a time you failed big and it didn't in fact lead to anything positive, or a time when everyone laughed in your face for even trying. Can't find any proof? Funny that. It's like these stories are not really real…

Next, write a list of things you have achieved in the last six months, year, five years, whatever. Include times when things haven't gone quite your way to start with, but you've come out stronger as a result (those are as big a win as the obvious ones). Keep this list somewhere close by (and ditch the negative list) so next time your brain tries spinning you a yarn that feels like it's holding you back, you can refer to the truth and move forward positively.

MAKE BEING FEMALE A STRENGTH

There is no denying that women have a unique responsibility and opportunity to challenge the status quo, create a more inclusive society and pave the way for the next generation of female leaders to break free from traditional gender roles. But phew, that sounds like a lot sitting on our shoulders. That's why it's important to remember, you're not on this path alone.

By building strong communities around our stories, we provide hope, inspiration and support for women as they seek out their own version of success. Our narratives can spark conversations on vital topics such as gender equality, social justice and mental health, bringing change and greater compassion.

Through authentic storytelling we can confront prejudice together, educate others and advocate for a more inclusive society. And by preserving and honouring the stories of women who came before us, we ensure their legacies continue to inspire and guide us towards a more equitable future.

But back to the here and now. There's no denying that gender bias still exists in many industries.

As a female business owner, you may have a perception about what is expected of you or what roles you should fulfil. It's important to try and confront these biases head-on by challenging stereotypes and assumptions.

Share stories that showcase your expertise, competence and leadership skills, focusing on the quality of your work, and let your accomplishments speak for themselves.

You may also face unique challenges in balancing personal and professional responsibilities. Your stories may include experiences of juggling multiple roles or struggling to find work-life balance. Give yourself a break. You do not need to be Superwoman.

Set realistic expectations for yourself and establish boundaries to protect your personal time and well-being and share an insight into this with your customers. Remember that taking care of yourself allows you to show up more effectively in your business.

Frustratingly, society still often expects women to be more accommodating and less assertive in business settings. Your stories may have influenced how you approach negotiation. Cultivate confidence in advocating for yourself and your business. Practice effective communication, develop negotiation skills, and seek out training or mentorship opportunities.

Surround yourself with individuals who value your input and treat you as an equal partner – rather than trying to silence you when you bring new ideas or push back on things you feel strongly about.

Building a strong network is essential – not just to help your business grow but to help you feel supported and less alone (running a business can seem very isolating). However, your stories may have affected your comfort level in networking situations. Take me, for example – I freaking HATE networking or at least that's the story I like to tell myself when I can't be bothered to try! Now, instead, I actively seek networking opportunities to challenge the discomfort I've felt in the past and build a bank of evidence that tells me it really isn't all that bad. And, in doing so, re-writing my unhelpful story! Tell yourself it's fun meeting new people.

Remember, your stories really can shape your mindset and impact your actions. Be aware of any unhelpful ones (oh hi there, Imposter Syndrome) that may get in your way of brilliance. Reframe your stories to feel more empowered, celebrate your accomplishments and challenge any of those out-dated expectations on you. Embrace your unique experiences and strengths as a female business owner and let them give you the super boost you need to achieve your goals and live an awesome life.

PS All of this is much easier said than done and definitely takes practice, so don't stress it if it all feels a bit too much right now. It will get easier.

Are you ready?

CHAPTER 1
WHY STORYTELLING IS THE
ACE UP YOUR BUSINESS SLEEVE

I'M BUSY RUNNING A BUSINESS. WHY SHOULD I GIVE STORYTELLING TWO HOOTS?

When I started writing this book, I felt very strongly that it wasn't to become a theoretical guide to storytelling, or a pitch deck for why you should tell more stories. I really wanted it to be about how you write – and tell stories in a way that works for who you are and what you're trying to do with your life. But I can't get you to that stage without first telling you a little bit about why storytelling matters so much in the first place and – quite frankly – why you should be investing your precious time and energy in reading this book.

Let's start at the very beginning because, believe it or not, storytelling has been around as long as we have.

Story – the Evolution of Us

> *"You're never going to kill storytelling because it's built into the human plan. We come with it."*

> *Margaret Atwood*

I'm often asked why I care so much about storytelling. Yes, I'm a huge advocate of increasing the number of female voices in the world, but it's also because it's one of those fundamental things that make us human. It's one of the reasons we've been able to survive as a race. That and the invention of fire. And possibly Netflix.

Do you know what the first story ever told was about? No, me neither. But I can hazard a guess that it probably had something to do with survival. Like proper, life-or-death, continuation-of-humanity survival as opposed to our somewhat meagre needs for quality Wi-Fi and good coffee. But, that said, just like our ancestors, stories continue to help us make sense of what's happening around us, providing hope for a better future and showing us what we need to survive physically, mentally, financially and spiritually.

And that, my lovely friend, is why storytelling matters so much when you're a brand trying to attract the attention of your dream clients and help them understand the value of what you do in terms of their own survival.

Now you might be thinking this all sounds a little OTT. "Hang on a minute, my lavender scented candles smell gorgeous but they aren't really going to help anyone survive." But, and I'm sorry to say it, you're wrong. Sure, your business story is going to be a little different to the ones shared by our cave-dwelling ancestors who ensured we didn't all die out on day one, but think about what we all need to thrive now? Calm. Well-being. A sense of space. Tiny moments of joy. Suddenly, your relaxing candles take on a rather different role. You're helping someone achieve what they need to be able to face the world, even if just for a few minutes a day.

Stories made us who we are now. And your stories are all part of our continued success - and survival, one special little moment at a time. Why? Because stories are what connect and unite us. They inspire and motivate action, from leading political and social change to small acts like your clients buying from you or sharing your content.

THE CRAZY-ASS THINGS STORIES DO TO OUR EMOTIONS

Just like with data, our brains can identify patterns in stories triggering chemical reactions that tug on our heart strings and create an immediate emotional response more powerful than anything our logical brains can come up with. Because of this, stories help create order from chaos, organising information into understandable narratives rather than lots of disjointed data.

Recent breakthroughs in neuroscience reveal that our brain is hardwired to respond to stories as a way of connecting with others. Stories light up areas of our brain associated with first-hand experience and 'theory of mind'

– the knowledge that other's beliefs, desires, intentions, emotions and thoughts may be different from our own.

A study by neuroscientist Gregory Burns showed that when subjects hear stories told in first-person, so from the storyteller's point of view using 'I,' their 'theory of mind' region becomes activated. This stimulation helps us understand different viewpoints and recognise cultural values. Proving my point that storytelling is not a fad devised by bored marketers or a money spinning exercise conjured up by overpriced advertising agencies.

That lovely hit of dopamine we get when we hear someone share an inspiring tale that quickly gets us hooked – that's nature's way of getting us to pay attention. Dopamine also significantly impacts our motivation, memory and reward-response behaviour. All pretty important when you're trying to engage your dream clients and incentivise them to act on your message.

We think in story too. Like I said, it's how we add order to the crazy bat-shit world we live in. Our brains are constantly seeking meaning, picking out what we need to know to keep afloat and telling us a story based on stuff we've already experienced, how we feel about it and how it might impact us now.

Side note: unfortunately our brain is not always our best buddy. It can take what we've done in the past and how we felt about it and tell us unhelpful stories about what might happen next. "Remember when you tried something new and it didn't work and you felt really stupid? Well, likelihood is if you do it again, you'll feel the same. Or worse. Best not do it eh. You don't want people thinking you're a total wally. What would happen then? No-one will buy from you. Your business will go under. You'll lose your home. Your husband, children and your three cats will all leave you. You'll be left alone and miserable."

Dramatic much? Maybe, but it is unfortunately how our brains can work. These types of stories are often the reason we don't use our voice, feel scared about talking about ourselves or generally don't put ourselves out there as much as we're worth. If that sounds like you, fear not. Firstly, it happens to the best of us. Secondly, I'm going to be sharing some tips for managing those cheeky stories that stand in your way of greatness.

There you have it. We come ready made with storytelling in our DNA and we just need to know how to tap into it. This comes down to our understanding of how our brains work differently when responding to a story versus any other type of information or data.

Memory Like a Goldfish? If Only We Were That Lucky

Since the introduction of smartphones and countless time-sucking social media platforms, some experts believe our attention span has plummeted. There's every chance whilst you've been reading that, your mind has wandered elsewhere, something's caught your eye, a notification flashed up on your phone. Oh hello, you're back.

I don't need to tell you that we have a lot going on in our lives. Instant gratification technology, the sheer volume of data our brain receives (1 million bits of information per second, 100,000 words received daily … that is some b.a.n.a.n.a.s shit right there). It's no wonder we're maxing out on overwhelm.

We live in a super noisy world which, if you're trying to get yourself or your brand heard, leaves you in a bit of a quandary. If you've got something to say, and I will assume you have – that's why you're here – you need to find a way to cut through all the data and information overload, not only to make others listen to you but to make sure they remember you beyond their next lap of the fish tank.

Good Stories Told Well Do Just That

Stories fire up your brain, giving the little grey cells something other than data to focus on and sending signals down your neural pathways that say, "Oi, you need to stop what you're doing and listen to this." A brand story grabs attention, elicits an emotion and engages the people you want to connect with. And that goes for storytelling across all mediums.

Clever brain bits (technical term) like our sensory cortex and our limbic system are the engine room of storytelling; reacting and flexing when our brain detects a story and releasing chemicals to gives us all the feels.

A good story can trigger your brain to release cortisol (the stress chemical which, in small doses, is also what makes stories more memorable than boring facts and figures). And oxytocin, which promotes empathy, transporting us into other people's worlds through their stories. This enables us to feel what they feel and, in a business world, creates a strong sense of trust which is mega for relationship building and customer loyalty.

Different mediums and storytelling tools affect us in different ways. Take video, for example. Video triggers a bonkers phenomenon called emotional contagion where we unconsciously 'catch' the feelings of those around us. Ever found yourself compelled to tears as the lead character weeps on screen? That's emotional contagion. Similarly, when we hear someone speaking, like a narrator in an animated video, it triggers yet another spooky thing out of our control called neural coupling – an experience where our brain activity mirrors what the speaker is saying. Nuts eh?

For most of us small business owners, creating Hollywood-esque movies or animations is a tad out of reach, but don't worry. These emotional responses are not just about seeing images or hearing a human voice; it's your core story that really matters. When you are able to tell a compelling brand story (and trust me, by the end of this book, that's exactly what you'll be doing), people are naturally captivated. Whether it's the story of how you built your business or how your product or service improves people's lives, finding a unique brand story is one of the most effective ways to entice, engage and encourage your dream clients to build a relationship with you and your brand.

Why Your Story ROCKS When You Run a Business

"A good story helps us see the world outside ourselves."

Barack Obama

Sharing your story helps others understand what's possible – and all the nitty gritty, tears and frustration it can take to achieve success, whatever that means for you individually. For women, this is especially important - changing the narrative around success and showing the world what we're all capable of.

When Alexandria Ocasio-Cortez became the youngest woman in the US Congress, she made a homemade video telling her story about growing up in her community. Over 300,000 people watched it on day one, and she went on to win, defeating a man who had held the seat for a decade. Now that's progress.

You might not have political ambitions (and quite frankly, right now, who would?) but your story can help unite others to become champions for you and your vision. Just imagine the power your own story could have.

Give Your Audience Something to Be Part Of

I set up my first business before social media was really a thing. I was 29, newly divorced with an 18-month-old baby. All my friends had 9-5 jobs (and no children). None of my family had ever been self-employed. And to make it worse, I'd started to get panic attacks. To say I felt alone would be an understatement. Almost 15 years on, I know now that I wasn't alone. That there were – and continue to be – so many women going through the same as me. There just wasn't the platform back then for me to hear their stories – or share my own.

Storytelling is an opportunity to connect with your audience on a deeper, more emotional level that speaks to their inner fears and gives them a sense of belonging. Stories, quite literally, make our world bigger. They allow us to get to know people we will never meet and take us on a journey inside their lives, enabling us to feel and see what they see, opening our eyes and educating us to be better humans.

Stories help us feel less alone in our experiences, in our fight to be heard, to carve out a space for ourselves. Like invisible bonds they connect us around the world with other women who, on paper, are different from us but, under the surface, are exactly the same. And storytelling gives us a way to celebrate these differences that don't require money or resources. Just a voice.

As a slight aside, at a recent networking event in my nearby town of Bath, it broke my heart to hear from a young woman, just four weeks into running her first business, break down in tears because of how lonely she felt. All of a sudden, I was back there, sitting alone at my desk in 2009 wondering if things would ever get better. But then something changed. The difference? I was in a room full of women of all ages and backgrounds, arms outstretched physically and metaphorically, offering their support to this lady. One-by-one we shared our own experiences, gave empathetic advice and practical tips and provided a collective sense of hope, that no matter how bad things get (and they will), there is a way through. I wish I had been sat in that room when I first started out by myself.

Build Trust and Reap the Relationship Rewards

Who doesn't pick the best side of ourselves to show to the world, and why wouldn't we? But is this glossy version of you what others really want to see?

If you want your dream clients to buy into you, then you need to build trust. That trust doesn't come from pretending to be someone you're not, just because you feel you have to be a certain person to succeed. I spent most of my 20s and a good part of my 30s trying to be someone else – it really wasn't a nice place to be.

Stories show a more human side, helping others understand not only who you are, but who **they are**, enabling them to see their own hopes, dreams and fears within yours and creating the strong emotional connections that help relationships thrive. Showing compassion, empathy and vulnerability in the stories you tell, builds trust.

Spark it Up and Inspire Action!

In business, stories are all about getting others to act, whether that's following your social media account, signing up for your newsletter or workshop, hitting the 'buy now' button or even parting with cash to invest in your idea. If you've done everything right, hooked in your dream client, built trust and shown what their life could feel like with you or your products in it, taking action becomes a no-brainer. Stories are also a great way to get others to say "I pick you" – perfect for winning awards, getting your PR pitch selected by the magazine you've dreamt of being in or getting that fan-girl guest on your podcast, which you never thought possible.

You're an Awesome Leader: Stop hiding behind that bush

*"If your actions create a legacy that
inspires others to dream more, learn more, do more and
become more, then, you are an excellent leader."*

Dolly Parton

Who is a leader? Maybe you don't even recognise yourself as that yet but if you're running a business, managing a team (staff or unruly kids!!) or working hard to get an idea out into the world that you believe in, you're a leader. And with that status comes power.

Firstly, you've got the power not to be a dick. Secondly, as a leader, you've got the ability to make better leaders.

Check out any number of TED Talks and you'll see that most speakers share one thing in common – they're great storytellers. If you need any proof, check out 'Your Elusive Creative Genius' - a TED Talk by one of my idols, writer Elizabeth Gilbert. TED Talkers use stories to bring their beliefs and experiences to life, not simply for bragging rights, but to inspire others to go on and achieve what they're worth, which is kinda what I'm trying to do here too, just FYI.

I'm not saying you need to be gearing up for your own TED Talk but there's no harm in thinking about how your story might become the motivation someone else needs to be a leader like you.

SOMETHING TO DO:

Think about what permission your story gives others. Maybe the permission to follow your passion, rather than drown in the rat race? Or maybe it challenges something you have long felt is wrong in the world? Or perhaps it just gives others the agency to take a break and enjoy something for themselves, in the moment? Have a go at writing your answer and why not share it as a post or blog to help your audience understand a little bit more about what your leadership can do for them.

SIMPLIFY THE COMPLEX AND MAKE EVEN THE DULL, WELL, INTERESTING

Experience financial tranquillity. We specialise in numbers and stuff. Our team offers some kind of financial assistance, maybe? Let us handle your accounts and see what happens.

OK, so that's clearly made up, but you would be amazed how many similar messages like this I come across with both small and big businesses leaving potential customers in the dark (and then wondering why they never get any leads).

Here's the truth. Your customers don't want to have to translate what you do or sell.

The more questions they ask, the greater the chances of them misunderstanding your value or, worse still, missing the trick all together about what you do and how it can help them. Stories are a great way to simplify a complex message or bring a more human, relatable spin to your messaging.

Take the first-ever business story I wrote for example. I'd love to say it was for some cool swanky brand. But it was about mobile network cables. Can you think of anything duller AND more complex? Or at least it was until I got my hands on it.

Imagine the following scenario. Me, sat in a windowless room as a gaggle of excited product managers (is that the right collective noun? A plethora, maybe?) told me all about the length of their cable – ooh-er! I nodded at regular intervals, pretending to be interested but bored witless. I knew then and there it wasn't going to cut it with customers.

So instead, I plotted to bring the story to life by introducing characters (real HUMANS) and charting all the times they used the network during one day – going online to check if their train to an all-important meeting was on time, calling their mum to make sure she'd received her birthday card, texting a first date where to meet.

I brought to life something that before was just fact, and dull fact at that, and in doing so, created human connections – something for this brand's customers to grab hold of and be part of. We honestly don't care how many terabytes of data flow across a network every second, but we do care if that means we can make that call, send that email and connect with the people we care most about. And that's the real story.

Like mobile networks, maybe your product or service isn't what one might call glitzy or glamourous. But I bet it solves a problem for someone, doesn't it? And there, you clever sausage, is your story.

SOMETHING TO THINK ABOUT:

Have a think about how you make it easier, quicker, more fun for someone to do the things they need and want to do. Does what you sell help them connect with others? Does it bring them joy? Maybe it helps inspire new experiences or build confidence. What would be the impact on them if they couldn't do this?

Whatever you sell, whether you perceive it to be dull or not, there's always a good story to tell when you introduce people. It's just up to you to bring it to life.

WINNING HEARTS AND BLOWING MINDS

You know that warm, squishy feeling you get when you're doing something you know is right for you? Or you make a decision and your heart skips with joy? All that comes from a part of your brain called the limbic system – the home of feelings and emotions and, most importantly to you and your business, where decision making happens. How do you impact the limbic system? You got it, with storytelling.

Back to the science for a quick mo. What we all know as gut-instinct decisions don't actually happen in your tummy, but in your limbic brain. The reason they feel right is because that part of the brain that controls them, also controls our feelings but, interestingly, not our language, which is why we often struggle with putting our emotions into words. When that happens, we look to facts and figures to help us rationalise and understand our decisions. Funny thing is, our limbic brain is so powerful it can often overrule our rational thinking, leading us to make rash and often crazy decisions … like following our heart.

"What has this all got to do with me?" I hear you ask. Research has shown that decisions made by gut instinct tend to be faster and higher-quality decisions. And if we try and force our customers to make decisions to buy from us purely through rational thinking, they will almost always end up overthinking the situation.

Instead, you want to be telling stories that fire up the limbic brain and create a powerful emotional connection that even the most in-depth logical analysis can't override.

Having a clear brand story and understanding your 'why' will help you talk about your products, services and experience more authentically; you'll exude passion, and it's in this moment that real relationships with customers are built and trust is established.

Stop for a moment and have a think about the purpose of your story. Why are you reading this book and what do you want your new learning and kick-ass storytelling skills to help you do?

If your main objective is to create awareness of your brand and get your audience to engage with your content, you'd be better off focussing on making an emotional rather than a logical connection. Telling stories that your potential customers can see themselves in and bring their own experiences to, will trigger those lovely emotional buttons rather than trying to force people to make a logical connection with messages like, 'Buy from me and you'll be really successful.' Don't worry if you're not sure what stories you can tell – we'll get there.

On the other hand, if you're trying to nudge someone over the finish line to buy from you and you've already built that emotional connection with them, some hard facts may help. But – and this is a big one – you can still tell these in a story. In fact, stories are a great way to make data much more accessible. Customer stories and case studies are the perfect vehicle for this – you can tell the story of how you took the customer from A to B and how this impacted their life (the emotional side) whilst adding in a few key facts and figures to please the logical brain. Let me tell you a little made-up story to explain.

Switching facts and figures for all the feels

DISCLAIMER: For many of you (me included) the following scenario may be the thing of your nightmares, but bear with me.

Imagine for a moment that you're on TV trying to persuade the Dragons' Den investors to buy into in your business idea. All eyes are on you; beads of sweat drip down your face and you just know you're blushing. We won't mention what's going on with your bowels right now… What do you do? Baffle the investors with loads of numbers in the hope it'll make you sound clever. Or is there a different approach?

If you've ever watched the BBC's *Dragons' Den*, you'll know that the most successful pitches come from a combination of *really* knowing your figures and the market opportunity and having a really great idea that solves a problem no-one else has managed to do. But how do you end up in that room in the first place? How do you make sure whatever you have to pitch catches both the hearts and minds of your audience?

Well, buckle in. I'm about to show you how. And don't worry, for many of you, you'll probably never have to pitch in front of investors, but everything I'm going to take you through is just as important when persuading your customers to buy into you – and from you. Or even when trying to get someone to get on board with a new idea or strategy.

Let's get back to the Dragons. They're not known for their patience…

Imagine you're the founder of an educational app that helps to detect dyslexia in children earlier than any other tests, but you need money to scale.

What do you do? Pull out all the stops with your fancy PowerPoint skills: loads of slides, graphs, business models, profit and loss graphs… yawn yawn yawn.

Or do you tell a story about someone close to you, your son, your daughter, who struggled through school with undiagnosed dyslexia, causing them to withdraw socially, lose interest in learning, feel depressed and alone? And how, in your lowest moment trying to support them, you realised if only there had been a better way to test for dyslexia, their difficult journey could have been totally different. And now, all you need to ensure no parent or child goes through the same, is funding … and here are all the facts and figures, yada yada.

Remember, we make decisions guided by our heart. And then we look for the logic, the rationale, to back up how we are feeling. When we hear a story, especially when we can relate our own experiences to that story, it triggers chemical reactions in our brain that create an emotional connection. And it is these connections that guide our next steps. Sometimes it means we act impulsively when the connection is really strong. At the very least, the connection will pique our interest and make us want to learn more.

SOMETHING TO THINK ABOUT:

Have a think about how you would pitch your business, your ideas, or even what you do at work in your department to others? Do you lead with fact or emotion? What stories could you tell to fire up the heart-winning chemicals in your ideal client's brain? Think about why you do what you do. What realisations did you have along the way that have guided your path? What are your personal reasons for wanting to help your audience solve whatever problem they have?

Now or Never: Telling your story in shitty times

I'm writing this book in 2024 and it's safe to say the last few years have been pretty pants on a global scale. So much of what has happened; the pandemic, the cost of living crisis, climate change, bloody war, has been so far out of our control – and it's been really scary. What if we took our energy and focussed on the things we can influence instead? This includes how you choose to use your voice and the actions to take now to achieve your future goals.

Your story gives you the chance to define what success looks like for you now – and in the future. It gives you a sense of purpose, meaning and a clear vision to centre your efforts and hold on to, if the world knocks you off kilter from time-to-time.

Things change, needs evolve, the economy flies all over the place and it's likely, at one time or another, you'll need to adapt what you do. This can be unsettling. But knowing what your brand story is and staying true to your purpose and values, even if you have to pivot slightly, will help you feel a sense of calm, order and control in a world which quite frankly can feel pretty wonky and scary at times.

When times are hard, it's not a reason to stop telling positive stories. In fact, we should be sharing more. Throughout history, storytelling has been used in times of crisis to bring people together.

There's a quote I love from Paul Coelho which sums this up perfectly: *"The Power of Storytelling is exactly this; to bridge the gap where everything else has crumbled."*

Today, stories can be a great way to humanise difficult subjects, provide a sense of hope and togetherness and give a welcome break from doom scrolling. When Russia invaded Ukraine in 2022, stories of humanity flooded social networks. I turned to these, for example from activist and chef Oli Hercules, rather than the news, to get a real sense of life on the ground beyond the rhetoric and geo-political spins.

Here are a few tips for getting the right tone with your storytelling in times of crisis:

1. Don't be afraid to talk about normal things, including, if you're a business owner, selling. We want normal. It's grounding and comforting. Your stories will lift people up.

2. Be honest. It's OK if you're struggling or if you're absolutely nailing it. Talking about how you're managing will help others feel less alone. Sharing stories of success provides hope but also the permission for others to talk about their successes without feeling bad.

3. Be flexible. If your story is no longer relevant, change it. It's not some massive Tory-style U-turn but a sign you're thinking about who you're talking to and the problems they're facing right now. It's called reading the room.

Even if you feel you've got nothing to share right now, or you're not sure what to say that's relevant, don't stop using your voice. Keep on talking. Our stories are the one thing we have control over and they matter now more than ever.

PLEASE GOD, NO! NOT ANOTHER UNREALISTIC HERO'S JOURNEY STORY

Why the time has come for a more relatable take

Time for some brutal truths. Your customers are a mess. And so are you (and me for that matter). But not in a bad way. Just in a real way. We all have flaws, messy bits, stuff going on that doesn't quite make sense. When you explore these and find the wonder in them through the stories you tell, that's where the magic happens; comfort, community, acceptance, sense of belonging and, so importantly in business, connection.

I worked for years in corporate marketing and, in this world, there was just one type of story. The hero's journey. You know the one – someone has a problem; the big business helps them out and they go on to rule the world. A total, all-out success story. Now don't get me wrong, done right and for the right brand, this approach can work really well (there's a good reason Donald Millar's Story-Brand book has sold so many copies). But, for many smaller brands, especially those that are as invested in their purpose and wanting to drive change as much as they are helping their individual customers, a new spin is needed.

Tales of the perfect hero? Another person transformed from nothing to extraordinary without a smudge of mascara or hair out of place? Nah mate, we're just not buying it.

We are not perfect people. I am not a perfect person. We are all works in progress. Sure you can write sales copy that makes you sound like the elixir to everyone's problems in life ('buy my online course and make a million pounds in a week just like me' … sound familiar?) But it's not going to do a lot if your customers can't see themselves in what you are saying.

Hands up who remembers the Bodyform adverts in the 90s? A perky, attractive lady, rollerblading in the sunshine with her dog, massive smile on her face, all because she was wearing an absorbent sanitary pad? She was on her period! Let's be realistic here. The more likely scenario would see her lying on the sofa, wearing manky pants, feeling like shite and wishing the world would just leave her alone.

We're looking to gain fulfilment through a sense of achieving something bigger than just ourselves. We do not go through our journey alone. We're hyper-aware of the community we live, work and play in, the people we meet, the privileges we may hold and the absence of privileges for others. We know that if we want things to change, we need to change them. Plus, it's not dog eat dog anymore. We know we are much more likely to be able to make change when we come together.

We want to be part of a collective journey – not be a single hero out on our own – making a bigger impact through the individual choices we make. So, for example, if we buy something that's sustainable, yes it will solve the immediate problem we have but it also enables us to fulfil our moral obligation or personal passion to do what we can in response to the climate crisis.

We're done with unrealistic expectations. We're fed up of air brushed images, fake everything. Social media has burst all the barriers and we're done. We don't believe it any more. And why should we? What's wrong with painting life like it really is? Full of hope and possibility but at the same time a little bit shit. Good days, bad days, successes, failures, it's all what makes for a real life. We crave complexity and drama because that's what our lives are made of.

As storytellers, we should be showing our audience a world where more is possible. I don't think showing everything being awful would ever help you sell anything, but what's the point in going to all that effort to predict a future your audience simply could never see themselves in? Yes we're here to persuade, to lift people out of their patterns of thinking, elevate them into new adventures and ideals but it needs to be grounded in some reality. So sure, you can rollerblade on your period, but let's go for a giant cake and bitch about our annoying customers afterwards.

Juggling Heart and Hustle

So many small businesses nowadays (and some big) are purpose-led. Not surprising when you think they're often the product of the brain of one person (you!) compelling to do what you do for a tonne of different reasons, many of which, but not always, are linked to your own personal passion, values, ethics or a cause you believe in. Sometimes that reason is money. And that's OK. Not every business needs to start with a higher purpose – and if yours doesn't, please don't think your story is any less valid – it's realty not. I'm here for being real. And more money, having to earn money to pay the bills is as real as it gets.

Many of the reasons 'why' we do something are linked to the idea of contributing to a wider collective narrative. Take my business for example. Yes – I'm very much focussed on helping one woman at a time grow confident in their voice but the reason behind this is because more women need to do that – the world is a wonky spew of out-dated white male voices and we need to change that. I can't change it all with what I do, but with every person I help, I am getting one more new voice out there into the world. For my clients who personally have been impacted by gender stereotyping, pay gaps, being silenced etc, knowing that by working with me, and imparting money for my services, which I can then invest back in helping more people, is a bonus – they get to discover their voice as part of my wider mission to getting more women to do this.

The traditional approach to the hero's journey does not cover this.

And then there's the economic value of buying from small businesses, the impact of the labour market, especially for women who may have been unable to return to traditional work through family commitments, lack of flexibility, cost of childcare etc. Buying from a small business may well be individually fulfilling but we also do it because we know it's helping a wider cause. Again – collective narratives.

We need a storytelling approach that's suited to multi-purpose businesses where the product is one thing but the meaning behind it is another. One that supports stories that demonstrate empathy with real people rather than glorifying heroism, show a depth of understanding of what's really going on with them and ensure anything we offer to help doesn't feel out of reach. Sharing stories of real people going through real things and changing as a result (even if just a tiny bit) will help your audience connect to you. No dragon slaying needed.

So if you have a social purpose, feel passionately about a cause and are using your business in some way to make a difference to that, make sure you're telling your customers about it. And by doing so you enable them to connect their own values to yours, creating stronger emotional bonds and, like me, leaving them much more likely to buy from you and tell others to buy from you too.

Your ideal clients want:

• To know it's OK to feel and be the way they are

• To feel less alone but still in control – not for huge transformation but just that we'll feel a bit better in the moment (which can lead to more)

• To be inspired, but not by someone they can't relate to. Claiming you can help people make six-figures in a week is wank. We want to be inspired by people that share our flaws, have experienced the ups and downs of ongoing failure and success and have or are coming out the other side, in human terms.

Here's an example from the story of lactation expert, Nicola O'Byrne that she uses on her website. You'll see it covers all the three elements above:

"Being a new parent can be an incredibly anxious and stressful time. You're wanting the very best for your baby and this includes breastfeeding them. But not everything is plain sailing. And when things don't go right, knowing where to turn for advice that works for you and your family can feel overwhelming.

It's my mission to help more parents feel confident in the breastfeeding decisions they make so they can feed their babies happily and healthily without feeling they're doing it wrong.

I use my experience as a mother of five children, a former neonatal/paediatric nurse, and an IBCLC lactation consultant with over 30 years of experience in breastfeeding, to provide more realistic support and guidance that focuses on the well-being of the mother and her baby."

Like Nicola, your stories can and will help your dream clients get all of the things they need and want, but only if you stop sitting on them and start sharing them!

WHAT IS A STORY?

Now you understand why storytelling is so important, what exactly is a story? Is it something that happens? Nope, that's the plot. Is it something that happens to someone? Not really, that's just an anecdote. What about something dramatic that happens to someone? OK, so we're getting a little closer. But only if that drama ends in someone feeling they've transformed in some way.

According to Lisa Cron, storytelling whizz and author of *Wired for Story*, a story is how what happens affects someone who is trying to achieve what turns out to be a difficult goal. And, most importantly, how they change as a result and the impact this has internally.

Put simply, stories are not about the plot – the facts of what happens. They're about how we, rather than the world around us, change. They grab us only when they allow us to experience how it would feel to navigate the plot. That's why it should always be your audience that are the main characters of your stories – not you or your business.

The story lies in what someone has to learn to overcome and to deal with internally. So you have to know what your main character wants, what internal beliefs, misconceptions or fear are standing in her way, or you can't construct a story that will force her to deal with them. Take my previous life – I spend years working with massive IT companies, talking about how their big transformational technology made organisations better places for people to work. In hindsight this was bollocks. Proper pay. Boundaries. Respect. Diversity and Inclusion. That's what makes somewhere a fulfilling place to work, not automated finance software and that's where the story should start.

Stories also act to reveal things about us that we know but didn't know we knew – which is key if you're trying to sell an idea or persuade someone to take action. They build on your audience's past experiences and knowledge to make sure they're engaged and invested in what you're saying and open to adding more insight. This way they're more likely to feel like they've come up with the idea by themselves rather than feeling 'told' or lectured to.

Adopting a more collective journey approach vs the traditional hero's story, presents a unique opportunity for you to stand out – not be a sound-a-like. It's an opportunity to bring out your personality, showcase what's important to you and demonstrate your original creativity rather than leaving your ideal clients thinking, "I've heard it all before."

I love this simple structure that's like a toddler asking why, why, why? It's very much inspired by Lisa Cron (she rocks!) and adopted by me to have more of a small business flavour.

1. **What do your audience want and why?** Consider their emotional needs alongside physical ones. Why are these currently not being met? What do they want to be able to do and what does the future look like for them if they could do it? What do they believe in and how might this factor in their decision making?

2. **What's holding them back and why?** Delve into their deepest fears, their shared experiences which may be guiding their thinking, the physical things getting in their way, and the emotional.

3. **What are the external events that give them no choice to act?** What's happening in their immediate

world as well as the broader environment where they live, work and play? Why do they have to do something now? What will happen if they don't act now?

4. **How do they change as a result?** Remember – this isn't always massive transformation. It could be as simple as feeling a bit more joy everyday which goes on to help them achieve something else, to a complete new-sense of confidence, direction, focus. Just make sure you keep it real to what you're customers really experience.

5. **How does this benefit them?** Look at the immediate and long term benefits. Think about what they can do now, that they couldn't do before – and how they feel.

6. **How does this benefit their community and/or the things they believe in?** How does their decision to buy from you and the resulting change in them help others? What are they able to go on and do next?

To give you a flavour of how this would work, I've applied the structure to a rather fabulous small business I worked with in 2023, Tipperleyhill.

Tipperleyhill is the brain child of artists and best friends, Abi Tippetts and Roz Berkeley-Hill, who create every piece of their original artwork together. Yep literally. They paint together on the same canvas at the same time. It's mind boggling. Yet, as accomplished artists as they are, with a pretty impressive grasp of social media marketing, they were struggling with the basics; being able to describe who they are, what they do and most importantly why they do it. So together we set to work to figure out their story and tell it in their voice – not using all the meaningless and pretentious language they so regularly come across in the fine art world.

Here is what that story looks like using the structure above:

What do your audience want and why?

- Original artwork that reflects their individuality and brings joy into their homes.
- The confidence to enjoy painting without fear.

What's holding them back and why?

- Past experiences trying to buy art; feeling it's only for the mega wealthy or well informed.
- Feeling intimidated or out of their depth in galleries.
- Being told they were rubbish at art in school.

What are the external events that give them no choice but to act?

- Spending more time at home, for example due to remote work has made them realise the importance of creating spaces that make them happy and positively impact their well-being.
- They need another route to getting what they want; affordable original art without feeling snubbed or looked down on.

- They need to find something new to do to break-up everyday life, a creative outlet that refocuses their mind.

How do they change as a result?

- They get a smile on their face every time they walk past their new Tipperleyhill artwork.
- They find themselves more creatively inspired and motivated to explore their creative side.
- They no longer feel afraid to try new things and experiment with colour, style and fun.

How does this benefit them?

- Life feels more joyful.
- They're open to exploring their creative side without fear of judgement.

How does this benefit their community and/or the things they believe in?

- They actively seek out other artists and craftspeople, knowing they can access original, exciting artwork this way.
- They share their experiences with their friends and family, spreading the word and the joy!

I used the outputs of this to create a narrative to describe Tipperleyhill and the value they seek to bring to their customers.

Enter the world of Tipperleyhill. Where art is for everyone and creativity flourishes. Original art and quirky illustrations that bring joy, colour and a sense of fun into your home.

If you buy what you love, you'll find space for it. Investing in original art shouldn't be complex or intimidating. If you like what you see and it puts a smile on your face, that's good enough reason to buy it. We offer a range of original pieces to suit different tastes, styles and budgets.

Nobody said you had to be good at art to enjoy it. We believe art is for everyone, anyone can engage with it, with the right teachers. That's why we also run classes and workshops where having a good time and feeling uplifted by the experience of painting is our number one goal.

The great thing is, once you've done this foundational work, you can have so much fun getting creative with your stories. I love to create fictional characters as a way to bring a brand story alive and show customers exactly how a brand could change their lives.

Here's an example of what that could look like for Tipperleyhill using the framework above.

Meet Clara, a young professional with a passion for art but a disdain for the pretentiousness of high-end galleries. She dreamed of adorning the walls of her flat with paintings that spoke to her soul, that reflected her individuality and brought joy into her home.

Working from home, Clara had become acutely aware of how stark her living spaces were; she wanted a sanctuary, space of joy and inspiration not only to work in but to live in too. Yet, every time Clara ventured into a gallery, she was met with intimidating prices and snobbish attitudes, leaving her feeling disheartened and discon-nected. She browsed the internet instead but was left feeling uninspired with the same old prints she saw all over Instagram and Pinterest. In her search for alternatives, Clara found us, Tipperley-hill offering original paintings designed to put a smile on your face and lift your spirits. She also saw that we were going to be exhibiting at her local art fair the following month.

As Clara visited our stand one rainy Saturday, we welcomed her, as we do everyone, with open arms. As she gazed upon the vibrant canvases on display, she felt a flicker of excitement ignite within her. Here, at last, she found what she'd had been searching for all along – art that resonated with her soul, that brought joy and meaning into her life. With newfound confidence and a sense of empowerment, Clara bought two of our paintings on the spot for her flat. Each day, she now wakes up to the sight of colours dancing across her walls, a reminder that beauty can be found in the simplest of things.

Clara's decision to support our business, not only benefitted her personally but also had a ripple effect on her friends and family. Inspired by Clara's courage to embrace her individuality and their shared love of art, they soon followed suit, seeking out local artists and artisans to adorn their own homes. And so, in this small corner of the world, amidst the hustle and bustle of everyday life, Clara found happiness in the simplest of pleasures – a brushstroke of colour, a splash of creativity, and the warmth of a home filled with love.

The end.

THE GOOD STUFF TO REMEMBER

Stories help us make sense of the world, connect with others and evoke powerful emotional responses. In business, compelling storytelling helps you cut through the clutter, grab attention and build meaningful relation-ships with your dream clients.

Your stories have the power to simplify the complex messages (without trivialising them) and make dull topics interesting by adding a relatable, human spin. By tapping into emotions and triggering the limbic brain, storytelling creates strong emotional connections that build trust and guide decision-making.

Sharing your story not only shows where you've come from and your successes but helps others see what's possible.

Being vulnerable in your storytelling deepens connection with your audience, leading to meaningful actions (like buying from you and telling others to do the same) and opportunities to grow your business on your terms.

In tricky times, your stories can provide a sense of purpose, unity and hope. By sharing stories, whether personal or business-related, you can bridge the gap between uncertainty and stability. Embracing honesty, flexibility and a positive tone in your storytelling can help you connect with others experiencing similar to you, lift spirits and navigate through difficulties together.

Your audiences crave authenticity, reliability and complexity. We're all messy people and we're looking for stories that reflect that reality of life, celebrate imperfections and speak to the collective journey we're all on, rather than focussing solely on individual successes. Rather than get struck trying to shoe-horn your narrative into a traditional plot like the hero's journey, explore other ways to tell your story (and I'll help you do this in later chapters). Why not adopt a storytelling approach that aligns more closely to your values, speaks to the experiences of your dream clients and emphasises empathy and connection over heroism?

And finally, remember that a story is not just a sequence of events; it's about how those events affect someone who is trying to achieve a difficult goal. It's about the internal changes and transformations experienced by your main character (likely to be your dream client or in the case of your founder story, you) as a result of facing challenges and overcoming obstacles.

By following a structured approach that explores what your audience wants; their desires, their fears, their motivations, their resulting transformation and the impact this has on them, you can create kick-ass narratives that resonate with your dream clients and gets them to take action in a way that fulfils both your purpose and your business goals.

CHAPTER 2
HUG YOUR INNER STORYTELLER

"I just need some support from others
that have gone through this."

Liv, Content Creator

I married the wrong man – twice. It was two painful (and expensive) lessons in why doing things simply to please others or because you feel the weight of someone else's expectations, is never, ever, going to end well. Now is not the time or place to talk about my relationship failings but I am happy to share what I learnt – because it was such a big lesson, it took two attempts for me to finally learn it!

I'm a people pleaser. Fact. I'm getting better now – or at least I'm more in control of it simply because I've experienced the shit it brings. Trying to fit into someone else's mould, conforming to their ideals of who I should be, how I should appear, and what I should say or not say, shattered my identity. I lost touch with my true self, suffered from low self-esteem, and teetered on the edge of mental instability.

It took me six years to finally embrace my authentic self, on my own terms. I took charge, envisioned the life I desired, built the business I wanted, collaborated with customers of my choice, surrounded myself with supportive friends, and pursued the relationship I genuinely deserved. I seized control and worked diligently, accepting my mistakes along the way. My vision remains a work in progress, and that's OK because I know I am finally being true to myself.

I understand that my experiences are not unique. That's why I tell my story, to connect with those who are going through similar struggles, offering guidance, support, and a little glimmer of hope. Even when all seems dark, I want to emphasise that things can improve.

By sharing your unique story, you can connect with others and provide them with valuable insights based on your own experiences. In turn, they will support your vision, cheer you on, and remind you to be true to yourself. Because, remember, you are bloody brilliant.

Action – Consider the following questions:

- What do you want your story to be?
- What do you believe in?
- What do you want to be known for?
- What do you want to sound like?
- How do you want your life to feel – and how do you want to make others feel?
- How do you want to be remembered?

Jot down some private notes (no need to share this part), and then compare your answers to your current reality. If they align, that's fantastic! If not, don't lose hope. Consider this as the perfect opportunity to begin rewriting your story today. You have the power to do so. This is all about YOU.

STOP APOLOGISING FOR BEING YOU

One of the questions I get asked most frequently is, 'Am I allowed to tell my story?'

In the Western world there are no laws in place around storytelling. Yet, there does seem to be something unwritten which dictates, in our minds, whether or not we feel we can share our story. The reason for this is often fear and it's understandable. Sharing your personal side, maybe even some of your vulnerabilities, doesn't come naturally to everyone. Plus it can be really scary, especially if you've got no idea how others will react. Will they judge you? Will they laugh at you? Will they care?

The first time I shared a post on Instagram talking to camera about how I shared an office with my partner Tim and showing my followers around, I got a DM from an ex-client in the corporate world. He asked, in a somewhat mocking tone, if I was trying to be a social media influencer. Not gonna lie, this knocked my confidence more than a bit and it was a while until I shared something 'not business related' again. Oddly, now several years later, it's my personal story content that often gets the most social engagement. Why? Because it's relatable and my new audience value that insight because it helps them connect to who I am and what I stand for. (Plus we are all really nosy at heart and LOVE seeing this stuff!) And this is what your story will do too.

Another reason – and one that is a bit harder to shift – is because society, or maybe key people involved in your upbringing or early career, have led you to believe there's not a space for you to tell your story. That women shouldn't do that, shouldn't show off about their successes, shouldn't put themselves out there. If and when the trolls attack, it becomes our fault... "Well, if you will share personal stuff online, what do you expect?" Uhhh, respect maybe? Despite what certain parts of society may want us to think, having a voice and using it to champion things that are important to you, does not make you difficult. It's not 'un-lady like.' Nor does it give others the right to attack you for it and that includes your close circle of friends and family.

I've struggled with my mental health and from time to time talk about it publicly. The first time I did, my very private, very conservative (small 'c') mum emailed me.

"Don't you worry about what people will think of you? Do they really need to hear that stuff?"

Umm yes, Mum. If there are people out there going through similar to me and read a story which makes them feel less alone and maybe even gives them hope, I think it's pretty bloody important.

That's the thing. When we tell our personal stories, they are never really about us. They're about the person consuming them.

Say what?

Understanding this was a big shift for me in my thinking and helps me press send on a story if I'm starting to doubt whether it's right to tell. Maybe it will help you to think that way too?

So, even when the story is about you (and I'll come on to that in a minute), you need to always put your dream client or the person you're trying to influence and motivate front and centre. Everything you share needs to relate to them, the problem they need to solve and what they're trying to achieve. So waffling on about your many qualifications, years of experience yada yada, can go in the bin straight away. Unless of course, that really is important to your customer. But 9/10 times it's not.

Side note: Apologies to all highly qualified, university educated people with 20 years' experience – it's not all gone to waste. You just need to show your audience how all that great stuff is going to help THEM rather than just telling them how brilliant YOU are.

That said, there is a growing trend amongst small business consumers to really want to get to know the person behind the brand ie YOU. So there is a fine balance to be sought in sharing your journey, your experiences, your values and ensuring your customers are able to feel part of that world and understand their potential place in it.

A Personal Storytelling Success: Belinda Knott, Pothies

Let me introduce you to Belinda Knott. Belinda is a talented maker, working in the hills of West Wales. She's the inventor of the Cosymajig, a wearable hot water bottle carrier that went viral in 2023 and continues to be a top seller. And maybe most importantly for you, she's one of the best business storytellers I know, present company excluded of course.

I started working with Belinda in the spring of 2022 when she came on one of my brand story workshops. We had spoken the year before but like so many small business owners trying to juggle a zillion and one balls, she had struggled to make the time to work on her story. Even after our initial time together, and her sharing a very rough outline of her brand story, things still weren't quite slotting into place.

"My head's in such a muddle at the moment, it was good to reconnect with this work. Still feel a million miles away from nailing my story down," messaged Belinda.

"You'll get there Belinda," I replied, "There's so much goodness in what you've created so far."

And I wasn't wrong. Over the coming months, Belinda continued to tinker away at her story. She played around with different voices, mulled over her purpose, explored where she'd come from and where she was heading. Like I always say, there is no forcing of this stuff. For your story to truly connect with those you're trying to reach, you have to believe in it 100% first. You literally can't make this shit up.

Determined to make a difference to those who could really benefit from hands free heat, whether as an antidote to cold water swimming (incidentally, it was on such a swim that Belinda got the inspiration for the Cosymajig) or to provide relief from aches and pains, she took to Instagram and TikTok to share her story. It wasn't perfect to start with. But again, she tried new things, got feedback, and continued to refine her voice and her story until one day it felt like home.

Belinda puts so much of herself into making her products; her childhood, her family life now, the beautiful countryside she lives and works in, her passion for change and fairness in the world, that it makes sense that she tells her own story. But what's most clever is that every time she does, you feel like she's talking directly to you – your own needs and vulnerabilities, your own experiences. You quickly become the lead role in her story in such an effortless and brilliant way.

I also absolutely love Belinda's use of language and I was keen, as I supported her on writing the story for her online store, that we incorporated as much as this as possible. For example, a quirky turn of phrase such as, "Like a bowl of apple crumble with lashings of custard, my creations are the deep soul comfort you need to conquer the world," amongst clear and succinct marketing copy. This is a lady not afraid to let her personality shine through and her storytelling is all the better for it.

THE POWER OF YOUR INDIVIDUAL PERSPECTIVE

"There's power in allowing yourself to be known and heard, in owning your unique story, in using your authentic voice."

Michelle Obama

There's no shame in helping others see the value you provide. In fact, that's what marketing is all about and, if you want to succeed in business, you're gonna have to just get used to doing it. But don't worry, I am going to help make it feel a little more comfortable for you.

It's not enough anymore just to do a great job. If you want your dream clients to buy into you – and more importantly buy from you – you need to be showing them (not telling them) what your potential is and the impact you can have on their lives.

Frustratingly for women, talking about our talents, passions and expertise doesn't always come naturally. It's often quite the opposite. Over the years, I've worked with a lot of female leaders and business owners, helping them create their own brand stories to carve out the future they want (and deserve). I'm lucky to work with some of the most incredible women I've ever met but they all share one thing in common – even when we know we're absolutely kick ass at something, we don't always feel comfortable saying it out loud. We don't want our success to make others feel bad, we fear judgement and we panic. When someone asks us what we do, we use weird words and phrases we wouldn't normally to try and fit into a role we perceive they want to see. We might mumble something about our credibility or experience but in the hope that no-one really hears or questions us about it.

And to me, this is a tragedy. I worked recently with a senior leader. She was brilliant at what she did but always felt she was being passed over for the big promotions because others didn't really see her full potential. Not because she wasn't brilliant but she had fallen into the trap of telling people what they wanted to hear – focussing on their needs rather than showcasing her own talents.

This is why figuring out your story is so important. I worked with her to figure out what she really wanted to be known for and developed a story she could tell that reflected her ambition and her talents. And guess what? She got the new role she wanted.

I see women all the time not reaching their full potential because they're just too afraid to show that side of them to others. We understand that storytelling can help us connect and build trust with our customers, our team, our communities but it's easy to find plenty of reasons not to do it. Fear, Imposter Syndrome, not wanting to be judged – and I was exactly the same. It's much easier that way. But, as I've learned, far less rewarding in the long run.

Ultimately, you have control of whatever is holding you back. In the same way that you allow these thoughts in, it's in your gift to change your internal narrative and get your story out there.

SOMETHING TO DO:

Start to make the change right now by writing down one thing you regularly tell yourself that isn't true. Mine was that no-one cares about my story – turns out they do!

Now, write down what the truth is. Clear your mind of all the negative thoughts till you get to the real truth. Stick this up somewhere where you can see it every day and come back to it every time those niggling thoughts reappear when using your voice.

Despite what you might feel now or have been made to feel in the past, everything you've been through, all your experiences, your learnings, your mishaps, your emotional highs – and lows, they are all totally valid and are what make you YOU. The combination of all of these things gives you a unique view of the world that's 100% yours, and that view is of great value to those you are able to help (your ideal clients). You just need to be able to share it with them. And this is where your brand story comes in.

To get you feeling confident in the power and validity of your story, let's first explore the distinct qualities and experiences you have that shape your voice.

I'd Hazard a Guess You're Not Afraid of The Bogeyman Anymore. So Why Do You Still Fear Your Voice?

A couple of years ago, I was asked to speak to a group of A-level business and BTEC students. As a storyteller, this was the perfect gig; I'm always talking to people about what I do, so I sat down to write my talk. Bugger, I thought, as the reality sunk in. These aren't business owners I'm talking to. They're 25 years younger than me. What on earth could I say that would mean anything to them?

As I often do when in a tricky situation, I think, 'What would I advise someone else to do?' Well, that's easy; I would tell you if you use your own experiences to tell your story and speak authentically, people will listen. But don't forget to tailor what you say to the audience and where they are in their lives. And so that's exactly what I did.

I stood up and spoke about how I spent a big chunk of my life feeling like I didn't fit in. I talked about dropping out of university, walking out of my first (and only) journalism job and swapping a well-paid corporate marketing job for the scary freelance world. I also talked about leaving a successful agency I had helped develop, instead choosing to set up a new venture that I felt aligned more with my values and creativity.

Unlike the speakers before me, I didn't talk in corporate terms. I didn't say what I thought the teachers would want me to say or what I thought would make me 'cool with the kids' (just saying that goes to show how desperately un-cool I really am). I spoke from the heart, getting excited at one stage and leaping across the floor as I shared stories about my passion for writing and desire to help others like me. I also talked about my failures and their essential role in my journey. Yes, this made me quite vulnerable, but without going there, I think I would have been much less believable. And my less conventional approach paid off. Several students came up to me afterwards to thank me for telling it 'as it is'. I even had one of the other speakers comment on how refreshing my talk was and how it had made them feel they need to get a little braver in breaking away from the corporate mould when talking about what they do.

Some of us are blessed with a natural confidence. Most of us are not. And I'd include myself there. And then there's the self-awareness to really understand how we want others to perceive us. Even those of us who are quietly confident about their brilliance can struggle when it comes to showing up that way, choosing instead to hide their light. Others of us will try and second guess how we think we should be perceived (yup – I put myself in that bucket!)

In my experience, however, if you first figure out who your audience are and how you can change their lives with what you do or say, the rest will follow more naturally. Just like it did with me and the students.

You don't need to create some wild and wacky story that positions you as some Goddess from on high (clearly you're already that) you just want a story that shows others that you understand them, are committed to helping them and takes them through the experience of you doing that and how they'll feel at the end. Everything else you do or say acts to reinforce that key message making it easier to keep showing up because ultimately you're clear on why you are there and how you help others.

I will leave you with the final advice I gave the students. Don't be afraid of your voice. It is one of your greatest gifts, so don't squander it pretending to be someone you are not. If people don't like what they hear – go and seek out those that do – they are your people.

But What if I Don't Have a Story to Tell?

OK. Let's pause for a minute. I'm more than aware that there will be some of you reading this book still thinking you haven't got a story to tell. Or that it's boring and why would anyone care? Am I right? If so, this section is dedicated specifically to you, so listen up.

I'm going to put this straight on the line. If you've done anything in your life, gone anywhere, spoken to anyone, then you have a story to tell. If you've felt things, been happy, sad, scared, excited, there are tales inside you waiting to be told. If you run a business and have people buying and using the products and services you sell – hell, you could write a book (I am!).

So how about we all stop saying we don't have anything interesting to say and figure out instead just what your story is and how it can help others because trust me, it can. And I'm pretty confident, given that you're committed already to learning by reading this book, that it will.

Just in case you didn't hear me the first time. Every business has a story, even if you think yours may not be particularly remarkable at first glance. Storytelling is about connecting with your audience and conveying the essence of your brand and this is what this book is here to help you do.

So, even if you think your story isn't remarkable, take a closer look. Uncover the special powers you have that make your business different, connect with your audience, and tell your story with guts, conviction and purpose. Your story matters, and it's waiting to be shared with the world.

All Change: How Do You Know When It's Time to Update Your Story?

When you look at your website or social media profile, how do you feel? Is it like staring in the mirror, a familiar face smiling back confidently at you? Or do you feel like you're looking at a stranger?

Firstly, I want you to know it's absolutely 100% OK to update or even change your story. You're not physically attached to it nor will the world fall apart if you make some tweaks. In fact, I would question it if you didn't. Why? Because life moves on. Priorities shift. Customers want different things. Hell, you want different things. Maybe you've had a big life event that's altered the way you see the world (it does happen, so don't be alarmed if this is you). Or maybe you've just let time slip by without noticing you're not the same person you were 5 years ago. Any which way, it does no harm to re-visit your core story (purpose, vision, mission, values, founder story) and even check in with the other stories you tell – like your product/service stories or customer success stories. And if you don't quite recognise yourself – or your customers in them, invest the time to make the changes. Your customers will thank you for it, as it will make it much easier for them to connect to the real you and quickly understand the value of what you offer now and how this can help them solve their problem.

A Lesson in Changing Your Story – Helen Perry, online marketing legend and host of the *Just Bloody Post It* podcast

When I started working with Helen in 2020, she was known to her Instagram audience as 'Not About the Kids' and her thing was all about creating a business and life for herself that didn't revolve around her offspring. But then her kids got older. Helen's priorities shifted and she wanted her 'thing' to be all about the people she was helping to market themselves online. So she changed her story.

She dropped the brand name, refined her audience and started an email newsletter, The Switch, which remains one of my favourite reads. She ran courses for small business owners wanting to up their online presence through Instagram and newsletter. And she launched the Just Bloody Post It podcast. Her values didn't shift but the narrative around them did, the impact she delivered, the vision she had completely transformed, putting her expertise and experience right at the heart of her story.

Of course, just having a good story isn't enough. Helen worked really hard at getting that story out there in front of an audience ready to hear it and staying consistent across a few key channels.

But nothing stands still for long. In 2024, Helen's re-visiting her story again, reflecting on what her audience need right now and what she's wanting to provide. Because this is the beauty of our stories; they are not cast in marble. Not only are we free to change them as much as we want, I'd also recommend it, because you can bet your bottom dollar that your dream clients aren't standing still either.

Unsure whether you need to make changes to your story? Here are a few tell-tell signs:

1. Your audience has substantially changed.
2. Your story is no longer relevant to who you are now and the reasons you do what you do.
3. You've experienced a life event, a divorce, a health scare, a big move, children flying the nest etc, which has taught you new things, shifted your purpose or made you view the world differently.
4. Life has naturally evolved and you haven't had time to catch up.

SOMETHING TO TRY:

A good starting place for updating your story is always thinking about who your audience are now. Not who you think they are but actually who has bought from you in the last 12 months and why they've chosen you. Think about what the one key message is you want to tell them – typically this is around the problem you solve for them and how they will feel once it's solved. And focus on what makes you the best person to help them. Feed these thoughts back through your story and update as needed.

A Little Aside About Writing

This may be a little controversial – and I'm in no way diminishing those who make a living from being brilliant writers (me being one of them) but I believe that when it comes to running a business or leading a team, stories trump good writing every time.

We all have our individual strengths and weakness, and not everyone is a natural writer but we do all have storytelling in us. So rather than stressing about becoming a better writer, it's just about tapping into what deep down you already know exists within you. Plus, who said stories had to be written down? Before computers, social media or ink, stories were passed down literally through word of mouth.

If writing really isn't your thing, don't let it get in the way of sharing your stories. Think about how you could get your message across visually – think photos, infographics, hand drawn doodles. Or go back to basics and talk directly to your audience. If being on camera is scary, audio is great too; podcasts are the perfect place to share stories. Plus you don't need to worry about grammar and typos. It's just you, speaking to your dream client. And it's often a lot quicker to produce than written content that you might slave over for days to get perfect (which, incidentally, it doesn't need to be).

SOMETHING TO DO:

Tell your story to yourself out loud. It will feel weird for sure but the absence of an audience to start with will hopefully let you speak freely.
Don't forget to record it though - it might end up being the most brilliant story you've ever not written!

TELLING YOUR STORY IN PUBLIC

My palms are sweaty. I feel sick. I think I need a poo. Have I got time to nip to the loo (again) before they introduce me? Damn it. The intro music is being played… "Welcome to the stage, Hilary Salzman…" Damn it, damn it, damn it. Here goes nothing!

How many of you are familiar with what I've just described? Despite being brilliant at what we do, it's all too common to lose confidence when speaking in public. Normal yes. Fixable, yes – with time and practice, most definitely,

If you're having to speak in public, sharing your stories is a great way not only to bond with your audience but to stand out from other speakers, grabbing the attention of those in the room faster and making you more memorable. Before I share my tips for harnessing the storyteller strength within you (yes – it does exist, even if your inner critic loves telling you otherwise), have a think about the last time you spoke up in public. How did it make you feel and what could you do differently next time to show other women in the room, it's OK to have a voice? Because the more we realise that, the easier it's going to get for all of us.

1. **Know your worth and embrace authenticity:** To speak with confidence, it's crucial to recognise your inherent value and embrace your authentic self. Share your unique experiences, perspectives, and strengths. Trust that your voice matters and that you have valuable contributions to make. Remember, your

authenticity is your superpower, so don't be afraid to let it shine.

2. **Cultivate self-belief through self-care:** Taking care of yourself is not only crucial for your well-being but also for building self-confidence. Prioritise self-care activities that recharge and rejuvenate you. Practice self-compassion, set healthy boundaries, and surround yourself with positive influences. When you feel good about yourself, your confidence in speaking your truth will naturally grow.

3. **Prepare and practice:** Preparation is key to feeling confident when speaking up. Take the time to research and gather relevant information. Organise your thoughts and practice articulating your ideas out loud. The more you practice, the more comfortable and confident you'll become.

4. **Focus on body language and voice modulation:** Non-verbal communication plays a significant role in conveying confidence. Stand tall, maintain eye contact, and use open and assertive body language. Pay attention to your tone of voice, volume, and pace. Speak clearly and avoid rushing. By consciously using body language and voice modulation, you project confidence and ensure that your message is heard and understood effectively.

5. **Surround yourself with a supportive community:** Building a supportive network of like-minded individuals can do wonders for your confidence. Seek out mentors, join women's networking groups, or

engage in online communities where you can share experiences and learn from others. Having a supportive community can boost your self-esteem, provide valuable feedback, and help you grow as a confident communicator.

THE GOOD STUFF TO REMEMBER

Don't apologise for your story. Like, ever.

Sod your internal doubts (no matter how loud they protest) and societal pressure. Your experiences and perspectives are valuable and worthy of being shared. Even if you feel like you don't have anything interesting to say, remember that everyone has experiences, emotions and lessons learned that can resonate with others.

Understanding that your story isn't really about you – it's actually about your audience and how you serve them – will help you sit more at ease with any fears you have around judgement or Imposter Syndrome. Tailor your storytelling to your audience and focus on how you can change their lives with your message. Use your personal story as a tool to reach your dream clients, help them trust in what you do or create and showcase your talents and ambitions.

Don't be afraid to share times when things haven't gone so well for you, along with your wins, as they are an essential part of who and where you are now. Find peace with your uniqueness, knowing it's a superpower only you have, and remember your story matters, no matter how ordinary it may seem at first glance. Every story has the power to inspire, to heal, to connect, and to drive positive change, big and small.

CHAPTER 3

CRAFTING EPIC NARRATIVES: YOUR BRAND'S ONE-OF-A-KIND VOICE

You're standing in a room of strangers. On one side there's a crowd of people who, on paper, are just as brilliant, just as experienced, just as qualified as you. And on the other, a whole bunch of your dream clients, all with the same problem to solve and lots of money to spend doing to.

It's noisy. You can't hear yourself think. Everyone is trying to get each other's attention.

And then the spotlight turns to you. You've got 30 seconds to tell the people with the cash, why they should pick you, over all the others in the room? What do you say?

Can you confidently tell the room what you stand for and how that's going to help them achieve what they need? Or do you struggle to find the right words? Worse still. Do you turn and run out the room?

Let's turn that imaginary room into Instagram, LinkedIn or Google. You've got even less time to impress and even more chatter to cut through. So what do you do?

If you want to attract your dream clients, create an audience full of engaged, wonderful people or even land that killer job you've set your sights on, figuring out your brand story is one of THE most important things you can do. But like a lot of important things, it's not always the easiest. But don't worry, this is all about to change.

BRAND STORY OR BUSINESS STORIES? WHAT'S THE DIFFERENCE AND HOW AND WHEN SHOULD YOU USE THEM?

A clear understanding of why you do what you do makes it easier to talk about yourself consistently, in a way that resonates with your customers and enables them to connect to who you are and what matters to you.

Your brand story should give your audience an idea of who you are, what you stand for and why that matters to them. It explains your purpose and how you're achieving your vision and sets out your values along with proof points/evidence to show how you uphold them.

Your brand story connects your audience to you on a deeper, more emotional level beyond just the products/services you sell. Helping them see how you add value to their own purpose and the impact you will make, not just on them, but on the wider world they believe in.

Writing it all down will also make it easier for you to learn it; giving you the confidence to own it and tell it on repeat. You won't have to keep re-inventing it every time you want to create and tell a business story.

Now, when we talk about brand stories and business stories, it's important to understand that they are related but distinct concepts. Let's start by defining each term.

A brand story is the narrative that conveys your values, purpose, and mission to your ideal customers and any other stakeholders, like investors. It's a way to establish an emotional connection with your audience and differentiate yourself in the market. Your brand story focuses on the 'why' behind your business, answering questions like, "What motivated the founders to start this company?" or "What problem are we trying to solve?"

For example, let's consider a totally made up company I like to call 'Healthy Bites.' The brand story for Healthy Bites revolves around the founder, a lovely lady called Jennifer's personal struggle with unhealthy eating habits and her subsequent desire to provide nutritious and convenient food options for busy individuals. Jennifer's brand story aims to evoke emotions and create a sense of connection with health-conscious customers who share similar values to her.

Business stories are more about the everyday 'what' and 'how' of a business. Business stories highlight achievements, challenges, and milestones along your businesses' journey. This may include stories about developing new products, going into different markets, customer success, or lessons learned from failures.

Let's go back to my example. While the brand story of Healthy Bites tells us why the business exists and Jennifer's commitment to healthy eating, a business story might involve her journey from a small kitchen-based start-up to a nationally recognised brand. It could include stories about how she sources organic ingredients, develops unique recipes, and establishes partnerships with retailers.

Why are Both Brand Stories and Business Stories Important?

Your brand story helps create an emotional connection with your ideal client, building trust and loyalty. It sets a foundation for your business's reputation and helps others understand the values behind your products or services. On the other hand, business stories provide transparency and authenticity, demonstrating your business's ability to overcome challenges and deliver on its promises.

The most successful businesses often have a strong alignment between their brand story and their business story. When these narratives complement each other, it creates a powerful and consistent message that resonates with customers. However, it's essential to ensure that these stories remain authentic and reflect the reality of what your business does.

Figuring Out Your Brand Story May Be the Best Thing You Do this Year for Your Business...

This might not be what you want to hear but I tied myself up in knots writing my brand story. That doesn't mean I'm not brilliant at helping others write theirs (the results my customers get speak for themselves) but it does mean I'm human after all...

It's really hard. Mainly, I think, because we're just not used to talking about ourselves or sharing what we really believe in deep down. And like a lot of things when you're running a business, when something feels tough to do it can often plummet off the bottom of your to-do list.

But we're going to change that. Together. Step by step.

Important note: To make it even easier for you to work through this, you can download my printable *She Roars* story framework from www.theroarofherstory.com

And trust me when I say it will be worth your while. Investing the time to figure out your brand story is like laying the foundations of a house. If you build on sand, it's likely to shift over time, causing all manner of problems; cracks, holes, leaks; all things that will cost more in the long term to fix. But if you build on something solid, no matter what your house ends up looking like, how many extra rooms you add on, what colour you paint the walls, the only way is up.

Let's start by looking at how you describe yourself – it could be your About Me page on your website, your

LinkedIn profile or even your Instagram bio. I would hazard a guess that it talks a lot about you (I mean, why wouldn't it?) and tells people things like how many years you've been doing what you do, where you studied, others jobs you've had. All great. If you're writing a CV. But you're not. You're telling a story that you want others to connect to. Do they really care that you did an Open University course in Zoology in 2001?

Unlike your CV, your personal brand story doesn't just tell people where you've been, it tells them what you've learned along the way that could HELP THEM solve their problem. And it tells them where you're heading so they can come along too.

By helping others understand who you really are and why you do what you do, you're creating all those magical emotional connections. If you stay true to your story, your audience will gain trust and you'll have a much more rewarding relationship.

By defining what success looks and feels like for you in the future, you're also creating something for you, helping you fulfil your sense of purpose and add meaning to what you do, which is great for those days when you're ready to pack it all in!

And it helps you stand out – your audience will be attracted to someone saying something different, especially when they can see themselves in your story – like holding a mirror up.

And please, no kidding yourself that you don't need a brand story because you're too small, too new, or because you don't run a business. Some of the most interesting brand stories I've worked on have been for women working in corporate roles looking to take the next step in their career and land the jobs they truly deserve.

Jargon Buster – the Difference Between Purpose, Vision, Mission and Values

Purpose: Your purpose is the reason you exist and the thing that motivates you. It's the essence that guides your actions and decisions, providing a sense of meaning and direction. It transcends specific goals and objectives and goes beyond money making, reflecting the larger impact you want to make on the world.

Vision: Your vision is a compelling and aspirational statement that paints a vivid picture of what future success looks like for you, and provides inspiration and direction as you grow your business. While purpose provides the 'why,' vision answers the question, "What do you want to achieve?" Your vision should be bold, inspiring and future-looking. It should motivate you for greatness (so don't be modest), overcome obstacles and push boundaries.

Mission: Your mission statement should focus on the specific actions and strategies you undertake every day to fulfil your purpose and achieve your vision. It should outline your core activities, target audience and unique value proposition that sets you apart.

Values: Your values are the guiding principles that shape how you behave, the decisions you make, and as you grow and if you take on staff, the culture of your business. Your values should reflect what's important to you and how you want to treat others – and be treated yourself. While purpose, vision and mission are future-facing, your values are grounded in the present and are 100% non-negotiable.

FIGURING OUT YOUR PURPOSE

Or how to create a consistent and compelling reason for people to listen to you

If someone had asked me 10 years ago what my purpose was, I would have spiralled into some sort of existential crisis. Why am I here? I don't know. But the truth is, brand purpose, your story about why you do what you do, is nowhere near as complex to figure out than you might think. It's simply a way to show others that you're more than the things you do or sell. You have a purpose and it's bigger than just making money. Or maybe it's not. And that's fine too.

When outdoor clothing company Patagonia say, "We're in business to save our home planet," girl do they mean it. They epitomise what it means to be a purpose-led brand and demonstrate it relentlessly – like handing over

98% of the business to a collective they set up to fight the climate crisis.

Interestingly, Patagonia always tell this story of environmental activism ahead of their brand or product… It's like the sales just come. Funny that.

Imagine, telling the story of what really matters to you and what you're doing about it…and poof, all of a sudden you've got an engaged audience, committed to working with you and sharing your great work with others.

OK, so reality check – none of that happens overnight. But having a clear sense of purpose and talking about it does make a big difference. Why? Because your audience want to connect emotionally with someone who shares their ideals, their values, their view of the world. In fact, as consumers, we now actively seek out brands that stand for the same issues we're passionate about. And as social consciousness has grown, we now care just as much about the impact of a brand as we do the products.

You may not be a multi-national brand (yet) but in the words of Patagonia's founder Yvon, "You have to start right from the beginning." So let's start by getting it right, right now.

SOMETHING TO DO:

I want you to think about the following three questions and jot down whatever comes first into your mind. Try not to overthink it (easier said than done, I know. So maybe set yourself a time limit to work on this – like an actual alarm!)

How and why did you start your business?

- What was happening in your life at the time?
- What problem did you need to solve?
- Did you have a deep rooted belief in something which guided your path?

What do you believe in?

- What do you stand for and against?
- What gets you excited about what you do or what you could do in the future?
- What do you enable your audience and customers to do?

What are you setting out to do?

- Bring joy to others?
- Enable connection?
- Inspire experience?
- Evoke pride and confidence?
- Impact society?
- Something else?

Take a look back through your answers. What's the thing that connects them all, the golden thread, if you will, the thing that gives you butterflies when you see it? That's your purpose. Write it down and keep it somewhere safe, as we will come back to it.

One word of warning – your purpose is yours and yours alone. Don't feel the pressure to come up with something clever or overly worthy if that's not what you're really about. As I said earlier, making a difference to one person when they need it the most is just as valid as changing the entire world.

I absolutely love this simplicity of social media consultant SJ Thompson's purpose: "To get shit done. For my clients and myself." And you can't say fairer than that.

Still Struggling? How about finding things you want to punch?

If you're finding it hard to think about purpose, here's another, slightly unorthodox way of looking at it, inspired by the words of Nathalie Niño, author of *Leapfrog: The New Revolution for Women Entrepreneurs*. Think about what are the things that really piss you off? Now, I'm not talking about people who chew with their mouth open, I mean the things in the world that you strongly see as wrong.

So for me, I want to smack gender bias square in the face. But like the good pacifist I am (read: total utter wimp), I choose not to use my fists but to channel my frustrations into helping women succeed, despite the barriers we all continue to face, day in, day out. That's my purpose.

But if you're thinking, "Hang on a mo there Hilary, I'm a pretty Zen person and I'm not sure I want to punch anything," of course, this all just semantics. Being against something doesn't mean you want to rip its head off. It could just mean there's something that really REALLY bothers you in your world. And maybe, just maybe it's the thing that drives you every single day to do whatever it is you do. But equally, there could be no negative feeling, just something that lights the fires inside your creative business belly and gives you purpose.

UNDERSTANDING AND ARTICULATING YOUR VISION

Or how to connect what you believe in to the hopes and dreams of your audience and answer the most important question they will ever ask… "What's in it for me?"

If you want to feel confident that you know where you're heading,

If you want to feel motivated and inspired to keep on going even on a bad day and especially when life throws you all kind of annoying obstacles,

If you want to feel fulfilled, and understand why you get out of bed every day,

If you want focus to stop you chasing every brand new sparkly thing that comes your way,

Then, my dear friends, it's time to figure out your vision.

Your vision is a mental picture of the future; a flash or glimpse of what's possible but hasn't happened yet, the lasting impact you want to leave on the world. Vision is the thing that guides us. Makes us want to learn and grow. Enables us to live out our purpose and – possibly most importantly – shows our audience where we are heading so they can choose to come along for the ride.

There's a Carl Jung quote I love which says, *"Your vision will become clear only when you can look into your heart. Who looks outside, dreams; who looks inside, awakes."*

And that's what you're going to do now. Look inside your heart and figure out your vision. But don't panic if you still don't quite understand what that means.

Here are five questions you can ask yourself to get started:

1. What are the hopes and dreams for your business (or, if you're not a business owner, think about your own career or family life)?

2. What is the problem you're solving for the greater good and what impact will this have? For example, maybe you've created an alternative product that's re-usable, solving the problem of single use products going to landfill, reducing the impact on the environment and doing your bit to address the climate crisis.

3. Who or what are you aspiring to change with what you do? (If you've worked on your purpose already – think about the villain in your world or the people/

things you're against – how do you impact/change them?)

4. How do you want your vision to make people feel? What do you hope it will make them do or think?

5. What motivates you to achieve your vision? What thoughts or beliefs are going to keep you going, even when times are hard?

One final point – we, especially women, are inclined to play down our vision – maybe out of fear of judgement or because we don't feel we have the right to take up space. But that's nonsense. You have as much right as the next person to dream big. Use your vision to show your audience that you mean business and create a world that they want to be part of.

Here are some vision statements from some of the female-led businesses I've had the pleasure of working with. I hope they inspire you as much as they do me.

> *Laura Matthews, Laura Matthews Nutrition*
>
> "I believe in a world where all children have access to nutritionally balanced, tasty and fun food."
>
> *Beckie Rogers, Harth Chocolate*
>
> "Our vision is to set a path for change, defining our place in the landscape of artisan chocolate with a new feminine energy and creative originality that others will follow."

Julie Williams, Lighting Fires Executive Coaching

"I believe that everyone deserves the time and space to realise their brilliance and to find greater confidence and trust in themselves."

SETTING YOUR MISSION

Or how to act on purpose to deliver your vision

If your vision is where you'd like to get to one day, your mission is what you're going to do every day to achieve it. It describes how you're going to act on purpose to deliver your vision and – most importantly – imparts a whole heap of really useful information to your audience to not only attract them to you in the first place, but get them to hang around for longer too.

Let's take a look at everyone's favourite Scandinavian furniture company, Ikea. Their vision is 'to create a better everyday life for the many people.' Big, bold, audacious. Can flat pack wardrobes really make such a big impact? I don't think it really matters. It's a clear statement of intention – and makes it very clear who their audience is (the many people eg you and me).

Now let's look at their mission. 'To offer a wide-range of well-designed, functional home furnishing products at prices so low that as many people (there it is again) as possible will be able to afford them. Not big and visionary. Exact and specific. There is no question what they do day-to-day or how it's helping deliver their vision. It's clear who they serve (again) and it shows customers what success can look like for them – a lovely looking home that works for them and doesn't cost the earth.

You're hopefully already some way to figuring out your vision (if not, it's worth stopping and going back to). So now it's time to get your mission statement sorted.

How To Write a Mission Statement in 5 Steps

Consider the following three questions and condense your answers into one statement. Don't forget to make sure it's clear, concise and free of fluff - and the value to your dream clients is ultra-clear. Remember, this is about what you can do for them!

- **What is your product or service?** Be specific, inspiring and show the value

- **What is the problem you're solving and for who?** Define your dream client and what they need. Think beyond the obvious; what do they need emotionally, spiritually as well as their practical needs? How is this impacting their lives at the moment? What do they want to change and why?

- **How do your product or service solve that problem and how does the value of this connect back to your vision?** Think about how your mission addresses specific needs and get clear what's in it for your dream client. Consider what success looks and feels like for them, for you and for your wider community and the world.

Let's bring this to life with my own mission.

"My mission is to hold a supportive, non-judgemental space for women running independent brands to feel confident in their voice and learn how to tell stories that connect them better with the people that matter."

Again, it's clear who I serve (female business owners), I've identified the problem they face (lack of reward for their confidence and knowing how to tell stories), I've explained what I do (creating a space for them to learn about storytelling) and it links nicely back to my vision of a better world where we're all connected by the stories we share, regardless of gender, race or background.

And lastly, and it's a biggie – if you remember little else from this book, make sure this is etched on your mind: **Your brand story is about the people you are trying to help.** Therefore you need them to be able to see themselves in your story and understand the difference you can make to their lives. You're there to show them how to get there.

To help get your creative juices flowing, here are a few example mission statements from some of the brilliant women I've been lucky enough to work with.

Anna Peters, Evolve Events

"My mission is to make planning and hosting celebratory events a fun, exciting and limitless experience, where nothing is too big an ask and you feel fully understood and supported every step of the way."

Rebecca Crayford, Lifestyle Manager

"My mission is to help women change the little things in their life that make a big difference to how they feel."

Sarah Gallagher, Psychologist and MD of Purple House Clinic, Edinburgh

"My mission is to create a nurturing environment where psychologists thrive, finding fulfilment and meaning in their work that's free from the burnout culture prevalent in the NHS and fully flexible to meet their needs and values."

Don't forget – nobody really wants what you do. They just want you to solve their problem.

Customers want you to solve their problem. Fact. They rarely care about the specifics of how you do this (and they definitely don't care what you call it – despite how long you agonise over product and service names!) What they do care about is the outcome. And that may not be quite what you think.

Take a bakery for example. A bakery makes bread. But bread is not their outcome. Their outcome is you enjoying that bread and how it makes you feel.

Or me. I provide storytelling advice but that's not my outcome. My outcome is how confident in your story you become, based on my advice. Because I honestly believe you will.

When we share this outcome through messaging and storytelling, this is what is known as your customer value proposition. Simple terms – it tells your ideal client why they should buy from you over anyone else and outlines the benefits based on the problem they need solving.

SOMETHING TO DO:

Time to apply this to what you do. Grab a pen and consider the following:

- What problems do you solve for your ideal customer (this could be an actual paying client, another team you support, people within your community).

- Pick one problem as your headline message – this is your promise to them so I would recommend the problem which you think either the majority of people have and that you are best placed to solve.

- Look at everything you do; the service or product you offer and think about specifically how it helps solve that headline problem.

- Finally, think about what stories you can tell to show people that you understand their problem and how you are best positioned to help them get the outcome they need. Sharing how you've done this for other people is perfect authentic story content.

Congratulations! You've just written your first value proposition. It's perfect messaging for your website homepage, sales emails or promotional content.

DEFINING YOUR VALUES

How to set yourself apart from the crowd in a way that's more 'yes' than 'yawn'

Not gonna lie, when it comes to the values section of a brand story, this is where I see most of my customers come unstuck. Thinking about what's most important to you seems really easy – until you actually come to do it. And the temptation is often to rush over this section – coz does anyone really care?

Answer is yes. People do really care about them and they do really matter. And here's why.

A good brand story not only gives your audience an idea of who you are as a person but, more importantly, also tells them something about themselves. The most power-ful stories are like a mirror – showing them a glimpse into their own lives, adding value to their story and creating powerful connections between what they see as important and the things you hold dear.

In simple terms, people look to work with others or buy from brands that share the same values as them. If you don't talk about your values, how will they ever know. Sounds like a lost opportunity to me... Plus, you can use your values not only to attract the people you want to but also to repel those you don't. Genius huh?

Your values are the principles that guide you in everything you do. And, if you have people working for you or plan to bring them on board in the future, they also guide what you expect from others.

Here are my top tips for thinking about your values:

1. Your values should be yours – not anyone else's. This means not saying what you think others want to or expect to hear. Think about what really matters most to you:

    •   What are the things you won't compromise on?
    •   What do you pride yourself on?
    •   What do you hope others say about you?
    •   What impact do your values have on how you serve your audience and customers?

2. Don't talk about a value, like sustainability or diversity just because you see everyone else doing it – it will trip you up in the future. You have to believe in your values, live them day in and day out and, you

have to be able to back them up with examples and proof points.

3. Dig deeper beyond the obvious. Being honest, transparent, fun or working with integrity are all fine but what do those words really mean to you personally?

4. Think about how you can say what you really mean with different, more creative words in line with your own brand style. You can have fun with it – for example, rather than describe a client as honest and transparent, I used the words – zero shades of grey. What you see is what you get. Or just make them a bit more personal. For example saying 'we delight our customers' rather than 'we're focussed on customer service.'

5. And don't forget to tell your audience what these values mean to do them. How do they impact the experience of working with you, how do they 'add value' (excuse the pun) to their own sense of what's right and wrong? For example, I have a client who has a strong sustainability agenda and is working through the process of becoming carbon neutral. They plan to share their learning with their customers, making it easier for those that also have reducing their carbon footprint on their agendas. A great way to create connection, build relationships and add value – all before they've even mentioned what they sell.

If you get stuck, imagine you hiring you. What would be on your job advert?

A Word to the Wise About Being Truthful with Your Values

I bought some new shoes online (swanky animal print flats with a lovely pointed toe in case you're wondering). I'm not embarrassed to admit I'd been influenced on social media with claims of eco-friendliness – the only fully recycled shoe on the market etc. I put in my card details and just like that, the shoes appeared a few days later. And they looked AMAZING. But there was just one small hitch.

Interested on how one goes about making my shoes so eco-friendly, I decided to do a bit of digging (hello Google, my old friend). Hold up, what's this? Sweat shops? Child labour? Oh my god, what have I done? Suffice to say I've never bought from that brand again and regularly tell this story where I do actually mention them by name (best I don't do it in print but feel free to ask me if we ever meet).

And that's the thing. When there are so many different choices on offer to us as consumers, we need to find a way to filter our options. And it's the same for your dream clients.

New Harris Poll research commissioned by Google Cloud in 2022 shows that 82% of shoppers want a consumer brand's values to align with their own, and they'll vote with their wallet if they don't feel a match. Three-quarters of shoppers reported parting ways with a brand over a conflict in values.[1]

---

[1] https://consumergoods.com/new-research-shows-consumers-more-interested-brands-values-ever

Your customers are increasingly seeking brands that prioritise ethical practices, sustainability, social responsibility, diversity and inclusion or local sourcing and contribute positively to the world. By embodying these values, you can differentiate yourself and attract those looking for alternatives to mainstream options.

When your values align to your target audience, it creates a shared identity and sense of community. Customers who value specific principles or causes find solace in supporting businesses that champion the same ideals, making them feel part of something meaningful and impactful. This in turn fosters trust and loyalty, as your customers feel you genuinely understand and care about their concerns, beliefs and aspirations.

And finally, if you are a values-led business, you tend to be more transparent about how you work, where you source goods etc. By openly communicating your values and demonstrating consistency in your actions, you can establish a strong reputation for integrity which in turn attracts and retains your dream clients who appreciate honest and ethical behaviour.

Don't Let Your Brand Story Fester at the Bottom of Your Knicker Drawer

I'm going to say this firmly. Please don't waste your time, money and effort creating a brilliant brand story to tick a box and then do sweet FA with it.

You see, your brand story is not something you write and put away. It's a living, breathing thing that helps your customers connect to who you are as a brand, the passion and beliefs behind your work, and the value you bring to them in solving their problems.

It can feel very personal and therefore is maybe something that doesn't automatically feel right to share. But that's exactly what it's there for. Helping you create those all-important connections with your audience and giving them a reason to buy from you.

So, here are five ways you can stop your brand story gathering dust and make sure all your hard work that you put into crafting it converts into lots of lovely new relationships and sales.

1. On your website. If you don't use your story to update your About Me, you're missing a trick (it's ready-made content).

2. On your social media – take the headlines – your purpose or vision and turn it into your bio to help people understand the value of working with you at first glance.

3. When you're creating marketing content; use each element (purpose, vision, mission and values) as content pillars and create stories to bring each bit to life – don't forget to make your customer the main character, not you and your business!

4. When you're introducing yourself at a networking group or online event – it's far more interesting than, "Hello I'm Hilary and I run a business teaching people to tell their story."

5.   When you're entering an award or pitching yourself for PR. Your brand story is a great way to differentiate yourself and create something that's not only going to get others to think, but make them remember you too.

TELL YOUR FOUNDER STORY WITH FEELING

It's highly likely that the problems you've faced that have led you to do what you do now, are the exact same that your dream clients are looking to solve.

So, for example, if I were to share my experiences feeling at sea with knowing who I really was, and as a result, being scared to use my true voice in case I would be judged or laughed at, I would bet my shoes that at some time in your life you've felt the same.

But it's not enough to stop there.

You can see yourself in my story, and it's grabbed your attention. Now I need to show you a way out. I would hazard a guess to say it's what brought you here, but you need reassurance.

So I share stories of how I came through, how I faced my fears, learnt to shush the negative voice in my head, and became, not only a more confident person off the back of it, but built a business, dedicated to helping others do the same.

Not only can you relate to my story, as I'm sharing the same challenges as you, you can recognise my ability to lead you through, as I've been there and done it and come out stronger as a result.

And this, is the key.

Take lifestyle manager, Rebecca Crayford, for example. When I first met Rebecca, she told me that she hadn't met anyone, including herself, that couldn't benefit from 'smoothing the edges of the things that get in the way of you having a good day.' And this was the premise on which she had built her lifestyle management business as a 'happier alternative to winging it.'

I knew that had to form the basis of her founder story, helping her clients feel instantly at ease with their own challenges knowing they were in the safe hands of someone going through exactly the same but who was just one step ahead of them in figuring out how to make it better.

Here is her founder story to inspire you and help you see how the theory is brought together in practice:

> "I'm happiest when I know I'm proactively making a difference to others."
>
> Running my own business was an intentional step to ensuring a balance between my professional life and the delights and demands of family life, creating space for myself and satisfying my desire to help others.
>
> I've always been interested in how people work and what makes them tick, studying human

biology at university before pursuing a career in marketing and advertising, working across borders and cultures and satisfying my love of travel simultaneously! Working in such a fast-paced environment meant juggling multiple moving parts, which my clients see as one of my biggest strengths when it comes to helping them manage their own lives. I'm Prince II qualified too, so project management really is my thing!

However, after having children, I needed a change. I never felt comfortable being a tiny cog in a big machine; I needed my independence to do something for myself and be taken seriously in my desire to run a business. And so I made the leap, initially working with people who needed an extra pair of competent hands to manage tasks they didn't have time for, before deciding to focus my efforts on women like me, looking to streamline their day-to-day to give them space and time to do the things that make them truly happy. As a pragmatic person with a scientific brain, I want to make sure everything I offer is grounded in practical support and advice. And in doing so, ensuring my clients can experience the immediate benefits of making small changes to their lives, something which differentiates my lifestyle management service from life coaching.

I'm still a work in progress, figuring out 'what I want to do when I grow up' like so many of the women I support, but I take great comfort in building a community of like-minded people around me that I can learn from as much as teaching them.

SOMETHING TO DO:

I want you to grab a pen and draw three columns. In the first write down a list of the challenges/ problems that led you to do what you do now. In the second column write down what you did to overcome each of them. And finally in the third, write down how that experience helps you lead your customers through similar challenges.

For every challenge, solution and experience, there's a powerful story right there waiting to be told.

UNDERSTANDING YOUR AUDIENCE

How to connect your story to the story of the people you're trying to sell to

When I first left the corporate world, I set up a business called Bright Black Marketing and I did a bit of everything. Or more importantly I actually did a bit of nothing because my offering was so vague, no-one ever really took it up. And when they did, it was a total mis-match to my skills and experience and, you guessed it, a DISASTER. But it did teach me a crucial lesson – when you tell a story for everyone, you tell a story for no-one. All that effort and hard work you've put into your story, that, "Oh my god, shall I share it? What if people hate it?" annoying chatter

– it all goes to waste if you haven't thought about your audience.

Creating great content – and even greater stories is all about your ability to speak exclusively to the people who want to buy from you. If you are too broad with your marketing, your stories will likely to be so generic and watered down they won't appeal to anyone. Your customers won't feel listened to and you might not be heard at all. And what a shame that would be.

When it comes to storytelling, being specific is your new best friend. But how do you go about being so specific?

Let's start by defining who it is you really want your stories to attract. Grab a pen and paper and follow the next four steps:

Step 1 – and trust me on this. Write down who you don't want to work with. If you're in any way blocked with who you are for, being clear on who you're not for, will really help.

Step 2 – Think about who you can deliver the greatest value to, who you enjoy working with and who needs what you do most. This could be your ideal customers if running a business, potential employees, another team or people within your community that you're trying to build. What are they trying to achieve? What makes them happy? What are their dreams? Their fears?

Step 3 – What do they look like? What makes them ideal? What must they have eg something very basic like the budget to buy from you, or it could be a unique problem, a stage in their life or burning desire to do something?

Step 4 – What behaviour do they exhibit that will help you identify them? Do they spend lots of time on Instagram, attend certain events, turn to business books for self-help (hello, I see you and thank you!)? What experiences excite them the most?

So now, you should have a good idea of who your stories are for. Give them a name and a face (this really helps to have in your mind and makes sure you just write for them, keeping focussed on addressing their needs rather than telling generic stories that won't resonate.)

How do you know what stories your audience want or need to hear? It's time to dig deep and understand what's really going on with them.

The more targeted your stories, the more likely they are to resonate with your audience and spark those all-important connections you're after. Understanding what's going on in your audience's world, how this is impacting them and what they need to do to achieve their goals or solve their problem is so much more important than telling them what you do or how brilliant you are at it.

Sound weird? Stick with me on this.

The 'So-What?' Test

How to make sure your stories are always about your audience

You've got three degrees, 25 years of experience, understand your industry and have a unique way of working. So bloody what?

If your customers can quickly understand your value, aligned with the problem they are trying to solve, they are more likely to buy from you.

With this foolproof method, you can put your customer value at the front and centre of every story you tell. And it's super easy. With every statement you make, everything you write, keep asking, "So what does this actually mean for my customer?"

Take my business, for example. I could say I write stories for small businesses.

So what?

Okay, I help business owners use storytelling techniques to market themselves better.

Yes, okay, but so what?

I help business owners use storytelling to attract new customers and create deeper connections.

Okay, we're getting somewhere now, but what does that actually mean?

Grow a successful, sustainable brand that exceeds your ambitions by learning to embrace your inner storyteller.

Boom – there it is! The point where you can't ask 'so-what?' anymore because you've already answered it in your statement. The value of what I do is clear – business growth and success, and you know what I do that will help you achieve it.

Your customers' minds are very hectic and busy. Showing the value to them upfront will, at the very least, catch their attention, allowing you to tell them more about what you do and how you can help them solve their problem.

SOMETHING TO DO:

Try the 'so-what?' test for yourself. Take a look at your website, social media etc, wherever you've described what you do. And now step into the shoes of your dream client and ask the questions – so what does this mean to me? Be honest – is the answer clear? If so, you've done a great job; go and get yourself a cuppa. If not, why not have a go at re-writing it and keep asking the question until the answer jumps off the page (or more likely your laptop or phone screen!)

How Do You Connect with an Audience that's Different from You?

My teenage daughter and I often have a clash of, how shall we say, opinions. Obviously, I'm always right (natch) but annoyingly she's grown up to be rather a strong willed young lady with pretty hefty views of her own (god knows where she got that from!). Such conversations usually end in a huffy, "Uhh, you just don't understand me" (her not me) and this got me thinking. Despite having been a 15 year old girl once myself, can I truthfully identify with what's happening in her world for her right now? And does it matter if I can't?

I work on a lot of brand stories for small and independent brands. You would be surprised how many business owners realise, when prodded a little by me, that their ideal customer is actually themselves. Perfect – you've got the ideal insight into what your customers are struggling with, how they see the world etc, because it's you (word of warning – do test your views once in a while, they may be similar but assumption is never a good thing)

But what happens when you're selling to an audience unlike yourself?

Let's go back to my teenager for a mo. It's safe to say although I can empathise with her problems, I can't truly identify with them. The competitive world of streaks on Snapchat, the pressure to get hold of the latest Charlotte Tilbury dupe make-up, the obsession with fake eye lashes. It feels on the surface like a whole other world (and one that I'm not entirely comfortable with). So what do I do?

Do I dismiss her seemingly materialistic challenges in life, simply because I've never experienced them myself and try and enforce my own understanding on her? Or do I take the time to listen and at least understand why these things are so important to her?

I tried the latter. I scratched a little under the surface of these seemingly petty concerns and what did I find? A desire to fit in with her friends. Pressure to look like the people she admires on social media. A disconnect between who she feels she is and who she thinks others expect her to be. She's excited for the future but she's also scared. Everything right now is big and overwhelming.

All of a sudden, our seemingly disparate worlds were feeling oddly similar. Actually we did have a lot in common. I could identify with feelings because although teenage life for me was very different, emotionally we had a lot of shared experiences.

The lesson here is, even if we can't truthfully identify with our audience – maybe you sell predominately to a different gender, different ages or people who come from a very different culture to you – we can take the time to understand them by inviting them to share their stories and more importantly, by listening to them…

…Because you never know where you will find the connections, things in common, similar world views, their value or ethics. And once you do, these are the areas you can use to build stronger, more trusted relationships based on shared experiences, fears, hopes and dreams.

Even if on the surface we are all so very different, peel back the layers, and you will be surprised just how alike we are.

THE GOOD STUFF TO REMEMBER

Whether you run your own business or work for someone else, developing your brand story is time well spent to make sure others truly understand your potential and why they should back you, rather than anyone else.

Creating a compelling brand story is all about conveying your values (yours, not anyone else's), your purpose (read: what you want to punch in the face), your vision (a mental picture of the future you see) and mission (how you act on purpose to achieve your vision) to attract like-minded souls, and spark that all important emotional connection with your dream clients. And your business stories act to highlight your achievements and challenges along the way in a transparent and authentic way, that others will appreciate as they seek to build a trusted relationship with you. Both are crucial for building trust, loyalty and differentiation.

A little personal note from me:

I totally get that all this might feel like a lot of work amidst all the other things you're responsible for both in your business and your home life and this isn't about adding to your mental load without purpose. Please trust me when I say developing your story lays a solid foundation for future success (think clarity of messaging, knowing your audience, being able to pitch the true value of what you do and why), as well as giving you a shit-tonne of ideas for content, social media posts, copy for your website etc.

Don't forget, you can make this process even easier by downloading my printable She Roars story framework from www.theroarofherstory.com

CHAPTER 4
OPENING UP: VULNERABILITY
IS THE NEW STRENGTH

ONE OF THE MOST SPECIAL POWERS WE HAVE AT OUR FINGERTIPS IS OUR OWN VULNERABILITY

One Friday night, I found myself a tad loose-lipped after a few glasses of wine. Across the table from me sat a woman who wasn't exactly a stranger but also not a particularly close friend, yet there I was, sharing a deeply personal experience with her. Why did I do this? Besides the Rioja swirling in my tummy, it was because she was going through a tough time with something I had experienced about ten years ago – divorce. At that moment, I had a choice: should I express sympathy, change the subject, and move on, or should I dig deep within myself and share my own story – not to overshadow her pain, but to show her that things can and do get better? I think you can probably guess which option I chose!

Let's face it: we've all encountered our fair share of challenges and adversities. To deny that would not be very ethical. Perhaps these experiences weren't our proudest moments, and they may still hold traumatic weight. You might feel a bit embarrassed, fearing judgment from others. On the other hand, you might take immense pride in overcoming obstacles or setbacks, no matter how difficult they seem. But deep down, you may wonder if anyone genuinely cares enough to listen to your story.

What if I told you that, just like my wine-fuelled conversation, when we embrace our struggles and share how we've triumphed over them, we can inspire others and give them hope? When you recount your journey, you become a shining example that navigating challenging circumstances and emerging stronger is possible – and surely, that's worthwhile?

Take a moment to consider how you could delve into your own personal stories as a means of offering guidance and hope to others. Being vulnerable and open about your fears, insecurities, or moments of doubt can foster a profound sense of connection and create an emotional bridge between you and your audience. This is especially valuable when building a following, a community, or a loyal customer base. Authenticity humanises your story and motivates others to embrace their own vulnerabilities, finding strength in their unique journey.

As you celebrate your milestones, achievements, and successes, you demonstrate that progress is possible, no matter how big or small. Sharing these stories isn't bragging; rather, they reassure others that change is possible and encourage them to persevere and celebrate their own victories. Perfect if you are providing a service, building a community of like-minded people or selling a product that can really impact and make a difference to someone's life.

By living your truth and being unapologetically you, you become an authentic role model for others. Your courage, resilience, and determination inspire others to embrace their own stories, dreams, and aspirations, instilling in them the ability to create positive change and fostering hope for a brighter future.

How Vulnerability Gives You Power When it Comes to Storytelling

I was lucky to hear Holly Tucker, founder of the UK retail brand Not On The High Street and host of the ever-popular *Conversations of Inspiration* podcast talk at the Podcast Show, London in 2023. She shared how she was, by her own admission, an instinctively private person. With a desire to promote the greatness of others, she was always more than happy to be the woman behind the scenes, until she started her podcast. As the host of this show, which explores the stories of those behind many of the UK's best-loved brands, Holly said she learnt to share more due to her guests being very open to her. Being vulnerable or, as she put it, "Sitting in the uncomfortable chair," came slowly. Still, she believes her growth as a result – and her ability to talk more at ease and share her own stories was a significant turning point for her. Holly is now a big advocate for normalising vulnerability – and so am I.

I'm not saying we should all be sharing our deepest, darkest secrets, far from it. But good storytelling is all about being real and knowing your audience as intimately as possible without slamming you with a restraining order. For some of you, sharing personal stuff may not be the right thing at all for your dream clients, and that's fine, too.

If you are, however, looking to build deeper connections with clients, being yourself and even pushing your comfort zone just that little bit further can make others feel at ease about opening up to you. This creates trust between you and enables you to have more meaningful conversations that inspire them.

To help – and I know this isn't an easy space for many of you – here are my tips based on my experiences opening up to my online audience through my podcast, *The Everyday Storyteller* and my social media channels.

Tip 1: When you talk about your own experiences, you'll naturally display some of the emotions you felt at the time, making it a much more real interaction. You don't need to overwork or overthink it – just tell the story and the rest will follow.

Tip 2: Conflict is a powerful tool. Don't be afraid to talk about times when you faced down potential disaster but succeeded in the end. Or even when you didn't actually succeed but learnt something pretty damn cool from it. There is so much goodness and value for others in that.

Tip 3: Make sure your story has a positive message; a moral or something you've learned, to inspire your audience and give them faith in your abilities to help them. Note – this doesn't have to be some god awful cheesy sales line. In fact. It should NEVER be some cheesy sales line!

Tip 4: Invite your audience to share their own vulnerabilities and give them a platform to do so. This could be as simple as asking your followers to respond to a question on your socials or via your newsletter or inviting a customer to come and talk on one of your webinars or an Instagram LIVE. Like Holly experienced, being part of the discussion about vulnerability is often an easier route, than just putting yourself out there alone.

When we run our own business, we do need to take risks, and that includes, sometimes, presenting a somewhat raw, more honest version of ourselves than we would typically feel happy doing, when and if the time is right. How much you choose to talk about your life is up to you and what feels suitable for you – and your audience. There's absolutely no right or wrong answer, but here's a truth I think you may need to hear…

People ARE interested in your life. Even if you think it's boring.

It's human nature. We're all nosey Noras who thrive on drama and emotion – the critical components of every good story.

Take a gruesome horror movie for example. Take away all the monsters and what are you left with? Human characters with real emotions; fear, failure, love, regret. The jump scares simply add to the atmosphere but it's normally the character's flaws and the strength they find to overcome them that has the biggest impact on us.

OVERCOMING THE WORRY OF JUDGEMENT

What if someone I know reads my story? And all the other fears we know are stupid but can't stop feeling them anyway.

Imagine this. You put your heart and soul into writing a brutally honest story that highlights just why you're so fucking excellent and then, urgh, someone you know actually reads it. Worse still it's 'that' mum on the school run. What do you do?

OK so this might seem like a bit of fun but trust me this is a real fear for many. I've felt it myself. And I've spoken to plenty of other women who feel it too.

The issue is that everyone has an opinion, and that opinion is not always helpful. Even when we do or say things that are most true to ourselves. Maybe it's those closest to you, family members, your partner, who probably through a mis-guided desire to protect you, may cause you to doubt yourself or adjust the way you talk about yourself and your dreams, to fit their ideals. Or it could be something a customer or colleague said to you once, or a fear about how people who work with you might react, if you spoke more honestly.

I'm just going to say this once. But loudly. **If people don't like what you have to say, go and find those that do.**

You're not for everyone. Seek out those that can add value to your story, not bleed it dry. And ask advice of those who have experienced what you're trying to achieve, not friends and family who have never been through it and can often, through this inexperience, be critical and doubtful.

Here's a short task for you: Write a list of all the people you're here for and all the ones you're not and stick it up somewhere you can see. Write stories for the people you're here for (so if you're running a business the people you'd want to buy from you) and ignore everyone else. Whilst you're at it, you can also ignore your own self-doubt that Susan on the school run might be reading your content … because who cares?

Of course, if the people you are trying to influence don't 'get you,' you may have to have a long hard think about whether you're telling the right story ie that's really going to resonate with them and what they believe in. But that's what we're here for.

DON'T BE AFRAID TO GO TO THE DARK SIDE

Why we appreciate honesty in storytelling

Two seemingly broken, equally unstable people get into a row in a car park. The guy, despairing about his life, reverses out of his space without looking. An SUV driver beeps aggressively, pulls off at speed and flips the bird. What comes next is one of the best TV shows I've watched in years and the perfect example of why going to the dark side in your storytelling can result in the most compelling, engaging and 'real' stories that your audience will really appreciate.

If you didn't catch Netflix's Beef first time round, I'm not going to spoil it for you but hasten to say the lead characters are not your usual heroes. In fact, for a lot of the show, you won't even like them. You may even despise them and their actions (there was lots of shouting at the telly in our house!). But trust me when I say you'll find yourself rooting for them in the end…even if it comes a tad too late.

But you're not here because you're writing TV comedies, so what does this have to do with your commitment to becoming a better storyteller in your business?

Honesty.

If all you ever do is paint a rosy picture, before long people will stop believing you. Why? Because we know that's not the reality. And it's fine. We can take it. We know that not everything is perfect because we experience this in our own lives every day. So stop kidding us that there is some state of Nirvana just waiting out there for us, if only we did the thing or bought the widget. We want to buy from real people telling real stories that fit with the way we see the world.

All great stories show the dark side as well as the light. But in your own business stories, this could be something as simple as sharing when you've made a mistake and what you've learned from it or a time when actually you failed, things didn't go your way and for a while, your future felt pretty uncertain but you came out stronger the other side. Or you can share the experiences of your customers, the reality that they face, day in, day out which is often a long way from the gold-coated lives that many brand adverts want to us to believe in.

If you are real and truthful in your stories, it's likely you'll get the same back from your audience, deepening the connection you have with them and helping you build trusted long term relationships, to grow your business or further your purpose or cause.

Action: Have a think about what stories you can share that really portray a truthful reflection of the world you're in and how this could help your customers trust you and your message more.

Tapping into a Collective Feeling

I regularly get invited to speak at business events, but there was one in particular that's stuck in my mind. It was a day-long conference called Enterprise Women in Business, aimed at women who ran their own franchise businesses. There to speak about the importance of personal brand storytelling, I shared the bill with some really inspiring people who, against all odds, had created amazing businesses. But nearly every one of them who stood up to speak, started with an apology.

"I'm sorry, I'm not very good at this."

"I really don't like public speaking, I'm so nervous. Forgive me."

"I hope I don't bore you. I'm a bit all over the place."

None of the speakers needed to say any of this. They were brilliant women, doing incredible things. I didn't care they weren't natural public speakers – this isn't why they were asked to talk, but it really bugged me that rather than shouting about how incredible they were, they'd let Imposter Syndrome get the better of them. Or had they?

In a room of almost 200 women, you can bet your bottom dollar every single one of them would have felt that nagging feeling of self-doubt at some point, the voice in their head telling them they weren't good enough. Was today the day they would be caught out?

By standing up and admitting their fears – rather than showing weakness, were the speakers in fact using empathy to connect with their audience and bring them into their world, just like any good storyteller would? Whichever way you look at it, Imposter Syndrome is a real feeling (even if the concept was invented by the patriarchy … don't get me started) and probably isn't ever going to go away completely. But there are two things you can do – and this is so important when it comes to being a better storyteller.

One, you can create a new inner voice capable of talking that little bit louder than your pesky imposter voice. Note – owning your story will really help you build up that more positive inner monologue.

And two, if you're speaking in public – an event, a networking group, a team meeting and you feel Imposter Syndrome creeping into the shadows. Call it out. Don't apologise for it but be honest. Try saying this instead: "There's a part of me that feels a fraud but I know you all feel like that. So I'm going to take the collective strength in the room to silence my inner critic because I know what I have to say matters and can really help you."

Sharing our fears in particular is a great way to open up conversation, because everyone is afraid of something – whether or not they want to admit them – that's another matter. But if you're trying to get under the skin of what your dream clients dread (in order to help them conquer this and move on to success), you won't go far wrong by sharing stories where you've faced your own fearfulness and won.

> Meet Bobbi Montgomery Heath.
>
> Bobbi was a client of mine and is now someone I'm proud to call my friend. She's a senior sales and marketing leader and she came to me when she was about to start a new – and somewhat daunting challenge. Promoted to lead a big internal change programme for the large business she worked for, Bobbi knew that the job she was there to do would impact everyone around her. Having experienced similar change programmes herself in the past, she understood that her teams would be feeling anxious and maybe even a little scared for the future, and rightly so. But, and it's a

big but, remember this is the corporate world. Standing up and saying you're daunted by something is not necessarily the done thing (it's one of the main reasons I quit that world over a decade ago). Bobbi needed to find a way to win over her team and get their buy-into her vision for change. But first she needed them to be open and honest with her about how they felt.

Taking Bobbi through the process of unpicking her own story, I stumbled across a fab anecdote from the beginning of her career when she was selling educational books door to door in America. Fresh out of Uni, and full of the fearless vigour of someone in their very early twenties, Bobbi embraced the role and didn't seem to mind when doors were closed in her face and she was told, quite often, "No thanks."

All was golden, until one day when she entered a dusty trailer park. Feeling the Virginian heat on her neck, she walked quickly to the first caravan and knocked on the door confidently. No answer but she could hear movement inside. So she knocked again. This time the door swung open and Bobbi found herself staring down the barrel of a shotgun. Apologising profusely but not waiting for an answer, she returned to her car and unsurprisingly burst into tears. But then, she wiped her eyes, got out the map and headed on to her next location. Afraid of what she might find, but not enough to stop her doing the thing that at the time, she loved more than anything else.

"This is the story you have to tell!" I exclaimed.

"No way," said Bobbi. "I'm not telling that. It's not very business-like."

"Exactly," I replied. And went on to tell her what I meant.

You see the people that were in the room when she first introduced herself, the people she had minutes to win over, they would have been expecting the usual 'leadership' presentation. Talking about gun toting Americans – well, that would have caught them off guard for sure and boom, she would have their attention.

Bobbi's story is a great example of her resilience and her ability to move through difficult times and come out better the other side, all traits that you'd want in your leader. But do you know the most positive thing to come out of her sharing her story? By showing her vulnerable side (she didn't need to share about her crying but she did anyway), Bobbi was able to invite those in the room to share their own fears of the change that was coming. Collectively they shared experiences and found common ground with a place to move forward. Pretty cool huh?

Action: Have a think about your own vulnerabilities and fears. How could you use your stories to open up more meaningful dialogue with your audience and ideal clients?

"Where there is perfection, there is no story to tell."

Ben Okri, poet, novelist and cultural activist

Hands up who's cynical when it comes to all those glamorous rags to riches tales we see touted around all over social media? Yep. I see you.

Keep your hand up, if however, despite you knowing they're too good to be true, you often compare your own stories to them, coming up with one single conclusion – your life is no way near interesting or dramatic enough to gain anyone's attention, let alone help you sell or create anything?

I know it's not just me that loves hearing about other people. Or that seeks comfort in knowing that others have had to make difficult decisions, overcome hurdles, fail, learn and fail again.

It's not sadistic. It's helpful. And I'd far rather engage with someone that has learnt something about themselves and the world along their journey than buy from an often face-less – and story-less bigger business.

SOMETHING TO DO:

Here's a challenge for you. Have a go at writing 2-3 paragraphs about a time when things didn't quite go your way. Share how it made you feel (emotion is a great way to captivate your audience), what you learned from and how it makes you feel now. Has it changed the way you do things now or how you help others?

Just to make it fair, I'll go first.

When I first quit my corporate job aged 29 to go freelance, out of sheer panic of not being able to pay my bills, I would take any work that would come my way. I agreed to do PR for a wine company (I'd never done any PR). It was a disaster. I was so stressed. I hid from my client. I did a terrible job and it really knocked my confidence. But eventually I got back in the saddle, taking one key learning with me – never ever pretend to be anything you're not. I'm now always upfront with my clients when I don't feel I could do a good job and, on the whole, my stress levels are much lower, my confidence is high and they love the work I do for them!

Right. Your turn.

AVOID THE TRAP OF VIRTUE SIGNALLING

I have a love hate relationship with LinkedIn. Actually it's not the platform I struggle with but the people, sorry, some of the people, that post on it. Whenever a story hits the news about struggle, adversity, injustice, a flurry of suit-wearing sheep (mainly men) jump on the bandwagon to use that story to spin their own motivational claptrap or highlight just how worthy they or their businesses are. But the thing they're missing in their mission for fast track at the pearly gates is that everyone can see right through them and worse still, are laughing at them.

What I'm describing is an example of virtue signalling; superficial displays of virtue and value, like temporarily changing your social media photo to support a cause which you have otherwise done nothing for or publicly expressing sympathy for a marginalised group but never donating money or doing anything to help them.

Virtue signalling in business, does absolutely nothing when it comes to maintaining authenticity and building trust with your audience. I would go as far to say, it can actually be pretty damaging to your brand too. Now, I'm sure none of you lovely people would ever be guilty of this but sometimes it's hard to know when you're doing it, especially if there's something happening in the world that everyone seems to be commenting on. Take for example, International Women's Day. Every year brands fall into the same black hole of shame by posting all about how diverse and inclusive they are, only for someone else to post their gender pay gap figures which tell a very different story indeed.

In order to make sure you don't fall into the trap, here are some tips to help you think about your values and stay authentic to what you believe in:

Be genuine: Ensure that your stories align with your values and actions. Don't try to appear virtuous for the sake of public perception. Instead, focus on demonstrating the genuine efforts your business is making to make a positive impact.

Focus on action, not just words: Rather than merely talking about your values, highlight the concrete steps your business is taking to address social or environmental issues. Share stories, initiatives, and projects that show-case real actions and outcomes.

Focus efforts on providing value to your audience: Share helpful stories, provide valuable products or services and engage meaningfully.

Promote inclusivity and diversity: Ensure that your messaging is inclusive and avoids tokenism. Celebrate and uplift diverse voices and perspectives, both within your company and in your stories but aim for genuine representation and inclusivity, rather than superficial gestures.

Be transparent: Communicate openly about your strengths, weaknesses, and ongoing efforts. Acknowledge any past mistakes or areas where improvement is needed, and demonstrate your commitment to continuous growth and learning.

Engage in meaningful chat: Encourage genuine conversations and feedback from your audience. Listen to their concerns, address their questions, and show that you are actively engaged with their needs and expectations.

Avoid overusing buzzwords and trends: While it's important to stay relevant, excessive use of trendy terms or buzzwords can come across as insincere. Use language in your stories that resonates with your audience naturally and genuinely, without trying too hard to sound virtuous.

Back up your claims: If you make any claims about your business's impact or values, be prepared to provide evidence or data to support them. This helps to build trust and credibility with your audience. And stops annoying writers like me slagging off your brand to anyone that will listen!

SOMETHING TO THINK ABOUT:

Have a look at your values we worked on in the previous chapter. How do you share these values with your customers? Are they on your website? Do you talk about them on your socials? Most importantly do you tell stories that demonstrate your values in action. And, it's a biggie, are they truthful? If a customer were to Google you, would they find any skeletons in your closest?

THE GOOD STUFF TO REMEMBER

Vulnerability is a powerful tool you have that can profoundly (and authentically) impact your storytelling. It is key to building trust with your audience and developing deeper connections with your ideal clients as people appreciate honesty and realness in a world that often presents an idealised version of reality. Thanks social media for that!

That said, it's easy to get caught up worrying about what people you know might think of you or fearing criticism from strangers, and this can often hold us back from being genuine in our storytelling.

By acknowledging and sharing your fears, you can connect with others who are likely to be experiencing similar feelings. Opening up creates a space for meaningful dialogue, enabling you to create the most powerful stories that resonate deeply with your audience and inspire action and change.

Sharing your personal experiences, physical and emotional, especially how you've overcome hurdles, is super inspiring for those that align to what you stand for and create a sense of unity and understanding. By being open about both your struggles and your horn tooting triumphs, you humanise your story and kick start others into feeling confident embracing their own vulnerabilities.

Ultimately, how much you share about your life depends on what feels right for you and your audience. Note - this is very different from what you think 'should' feel right or what you see others doing. There is no right or wrong answer. If in doubt, cast out a more vulnerable post, Reel or blog and see how your audience respond. Ask them if they'd like more or less of the same from you and use their reactions to draw out your own boundaries.

CHAPTER 5
EXPERT-LEVEL
NARRATIVE MASTERY

WITHOUT CHANGE, A STORY IS JUST A BUNCH OF WORDS

I feel the adrenaline flood my body, fingers curling up towards my palms, nails digging into my skin, searching for some sort of relief. I feel like I could faint but I know I won't. I'm fighting for breath and the short rapid intakes of oxygen make me dizzy. And then it stops. Everything aches. I can't open my eyes. I just need to sleep. The anxiety hangover has begun.

But I've got work to do. A Zoom with clients at 3.30. My team need me, I can't let them down. God, I hate this feeling. But I'm so lucky. I've built a great business. Why can't I just fit in. Be like the others. Be stronger. Care less.

And so it continues. Day after day, week after week, month after month. I make changes. The team is great. Everybody rallies round. They say it's OK. But I know it's not. Their patience runs thin. I can't afford another panic attack. I've got to be better. Got to be stronger.

And then. Nothing. I can't do it anymore. This isn't me. I'm better than this. I am strong enough. I care more and I won't ever change that. Determined to own my own story, I take the leap.

Every day I grow now. Stretching out my branches into new spaces I didn't know existed. The feeling, knowing I'm helping others like me, keeps my panic at bay. I'm happy. I'm me.

The end.

So let's un-pick that.

Like most novels, films, dramatic episodes on Netflix box sets, you can break a story down into three distinct sections; a crisis, a struggle and resolution. It's essentially the same as any business case study; challenge, solution, benefit is just a more boring way of saying the same. It's also what our lives are made up of.

In my story above, my crisis was my mental health breakdown resulting in regular panic attacks.

My struggle was me carrying on in a job, despite how it made me feel, with the slow realisation that I needed something new.

My resolution is where I am now. Happy to be helping people in a way that's right for me. Through my words, you saw me move from despair to being free. And this transformation of lead character is absolutely critical for your stories too.

SOMETHING TO THINK ABOUT:

Have a think about what change happens in your business story. Rather than just focussing on your own story of how you got here, think about your ideal client. What transformation do they go through, working with you or using the product that you sell? What's their 'crisis' and 'struggle' and how do you help them resolve it?

Note – a 'crisis' doesn't have to have Jed Mercurio levels of drama. It could be something as simple as a customer having to find a present for a difficult to buy for aunt that also needs to be sustainable and British-made, and you providing the perfect answer. The change that happens to your customer is moving from a state of panic and worry about not being able to please said aunt, to being happy and relaxed when they get a lovely note of thanks through the post from her.

Storytelling in business is all about how you connect your story and what you're trying to achieve with the needs, wants, desires and values of your audience in an engaging way that sparks empathy (great for relationships), a sense of belonging, ensuring your customers feel seen and heard) and, importantly, action. Whether that's listening to your podcast, signing up to your workshop or buying what you're selling.

INTRODUCING SUBSTANCE, SIZZLE AND STRUCTURE: YOUR TICKET TO BRILLIANTLY CRAFTED STORIES

My step-by-step framework will help you not only think about all the things that need to go into your story, but, most importantly, get all the thoughts out of your head and into a format which you can then use for content, whether that's social media, sales emails, on your website or even in person.

You can download a printable version of this – How To Write a Business Story in 3 Steps from www.theroarofherstory.com Work through each section as you read and by the end, you'll have your first complete story! Yay you!

Substance over style (the details)
- What's the purpose of your story?
- What sort of story do you want to tell?
- Who is the story about?
- What happens?
- When did it happen?
- Where did it happen?
- Why did it happen?

Story sizzle (the exciting stuff)
- What do you want your ideal client to feel?
- What is the problem you are solving?
- What's your wisdom?

- Were there any emotional highs and lows?
- Did anything funny happen?
- Could you use metaphors, analogies or similes to help you explain your story?

Structuring your story (bringing it all together in 3 acts)

- What was the crisis?
- What was the struggle?
- What was the resolution?
- What is your headline?
- What is your call-to-action?

Let's go through each section in more detail.

SECTION 1 – SUBSTANCE OVER STYLE

How to make sure your story has all the right stuff in it before you start writing it

Margot Robbie, Brad Pitt, dancing elephants, 1930s Hollywood excess, what's not to love? Well, in the case of the movie *Babylon*, quite a lot. If you haven't already seen it, you're the lucky one. It's 3 hours, 9 minutes of my life I'm never getting back and the perfect example of style over substance. It looks amazing, but the story that sits behind it, the things we can learn about ourselves watching it? It's just not there for me. And that's a shame. A story that's empty of all the things that make stories great. But don't worry, I'm here to make sure your stories don't go the same way!

There's something I personally find a little mind blowing; the majority of people who come to me for help writing a story have failed to ask themselves the number one question – "Why do I want to tell this story?" Sounds obvious, but trust me, if you miss this stage, you may as well can the whole story entirely.

Presuming you don't want to do that, here are some ideas about story purpose to get your brain fired up:

What is the Purpose of Your Story?

To improve awareness of something. Something you're selling perhaps, a free course, an event, an activity you're doing to raise money for charity?

To improve someone's ability to do something. Are you wanting to teach your something new? Give someone the tools to complete a task? Provide confidence and reassurance?

To inform behaviour or drive certain actions. Maybe you're trying to build a community, get others to share their own stories or come together behind a common cause?

To change beliefs. Maybe your story has a higher purpose? This could be as simple as helping someone who thinks they're not good enough, all the way up to driving big change in society, like gender stereotyping.

What Type of Story So You Want to Tell?

- Your 'why' story
- Your founder story AKA your About Me
- Your higher purpose story
- A success story
- A customer story
- A human interest story
- A personal experience

Getting Creative – The Seven Plot Types

Did you know that all stories fall into one of only seven basic plot lines?

Christopher Booker, author of *The Seven Basic Plots*, distils all storytelling throughout history into the following archetypes:

1. Voyage and Return

You're suddenly jolted into a new world where you need to face your fears before returning to your old world where everything has remained the same – but you're a changed person, rich with experiences and learning about yourself. Think *Alice in Wonderland*, *Wizard of Oz* and *Toy Story*. Great if you want to show your customers how you can take them on a journey of self-discovery.

2. Overcoming the Monster

Faced with an impossible evil (real or figurative), you go on a journey to overcome it through an epic battle, which you eventually win, and find yourself stronger than ever before. *Jurassic Park*, Stephen King's *IT*, even *Rocky* are great examples. Perfect if your dream clients are facing a demon in their lives and you can help give them the strength to overcome it.

3. The Hero's Quest

If like me you're an 80s child, Steven Spielberg's adventure film *The Goonies* is the most perfect example of this plot type. A hero or group of heroes embark on a journey for some type of 'holy grail,' could be happiness, love, or saving their family home from a greedy developer. Along the way, they face adversity and a string of tests and meet an unlikely character who will help them eventually emerge victorious. Think also, *Lord of The Rings* and any other corporate story ever written! Great if you want a simple structure to follow but try not to fall into the trap of making everything sound too peachy – your story needs to be realistic and relatable and that means talking about the hero in human terms, flaws, and all.

4. Rags to Riches

Any *Harry Potter* fans will recognise this one. A seemingly insignificant character who has faced hard times and is in dire straits, transforms into someone exceptional. It's essentially about the journey from struggle to success which may well align rather nicely to your own story.

5. Comedy

Rom com fans, this plot type is for you. Think about a series of confusing, awkward or comical events, probably involving a love interest, about people trying to win out but having laughable problems, finding their way. Think *Bridget Jones* or pretty much anything ever written by Richard Curtis. Maybe your own experiences building your business have been somewhat comedic? If so, this is the plot type for you.

6. Tragedy

Shakespeare's *Romeo and Juliet* is the ultimate tragedy but for a more up to date example, try *Breaking Bad*. Tragedy plots are all about the main character trying to attain something that's forbidden (or in Walter White's case, highly illegal) which leads them down a spiralling path of setbacks and failures, leading to a final tragic conclusion where more often than not, they end up dead. Tricky one to attach to your business stories, but could be used to highlight an issue or cause you feel passionate about.

7. Rebirth

Someone (your dream client?) changes for the better under the guidance of another (could be you?) because they are inspired to become a better person. *Shawshank Redemption* and *Groundhog Day* are worth a watch if you want to see this plot type in action.

This may all feel a step too far for you but there are a couple of key advantages to using classic story structure. Not least it will make it super clear to the brains of your dream clients that you're telling a story, triggering all those wonderful emotional responses and creating a stronger bond between you and them but will also keep your audience wanting to know more.

Despite my personal feelings towards it, this is why the hero's journey is so popular (someone has a goal and problem to solve, they meet someone that shows them the way and leads them to success) but there are also several other creative structures that could work well for you. My personal favourite is Overcoming the Monster. Netflix hit show Stranger Things is the perfect example of this – a community has fallen under the visible shadow of evil and they come together to liberate everyone from it. What would the monster be in your story – maybe societies obsession with beauty and the pressure this puts on us or something more simple like the constant juggle so many of us, face with work and family?

Creative Storytelling in Action

If you're struggling to relate how a business story could fit into these seemingly 'out-there' plot types and, trust me, I fully understand that – after all you are brilliant at what you do but that may not include creative writing – here's an example of a story I wrote. It was for a government-backed organisation that provides advice and mentoring for small business owners by partnering them up with big businesses. For the purpose of anonymity let's call them Business Brain.

Business Brain had been struggling to sell the benefits of what they do to large businesses but they needed to build these relationships, not only so they had a healthy pool of people to work with their small businesses, but also (surprise, surprise) the Government grants were drying up and they needed funding. The biggest problem was the people they approached had so much going on in their jobs, their own ambitions etc, they didn't give them the time of day.

If only Business Brain could show them how by partnering together, they could not only make a big difference to the growth of successful small businesses in the UK, but the whole experience could also be personally rewarding for those involved.

Cue a fictional story based on a combination of Voyage and Return and Overcoming the Monster.

Let's Start with a Summary of the Story

Remember – this is a creative and fictional story based on real-life issues, pain points and experiences shared by the sales and marketing teams at Business Brain.

Plot Overview

This is a journey of discovery for a man called Michael to find the answers to everything the world's throwing at small business owners and overcome the monsters of internal bureaucracy to save the economy and the world!

Helped out by an unlikely friend (Business Brain) and finding power in bringing people together (other small business leaders), our hero comes up with a plan. But wait, there's a monster to defeat first – the internal sales process!

Together Michael and Business Brain fight an epic battle and win the monster over. Michael returns home happy and enlightened, with a new understanding that he can achieve his desires and ambitions whilst also positively impacting a broader mission.

Note: Returning home is a useful metaphor for the personal end goals we all individually seek, whether personal gain, something more generous or a combination of the two.

The Full Story

Constant storms loom large. Strong winds sweep us off our feet before setting us down in lands we do not recognise. Uncharted, full of risk and opportunity, we want for one thing; to find our way home.

Michael's on a path to success, proving himself and ascending the corporate ladder. Yet he wants more. If he can get that recognition from his peers, that sought after promotion, he'll be happy. But the world is changing shape. The big guns need to look after the smaller guys. Not because they're any less capable but because they're the future. Michael understands by helping small businesses become more productive, the economy has a good shot of thriving again in the future, creating better lives with less disparity and more opportunities for more people. This is the mission he wants to associate himself with, if he's to get the accolades.

So off he sets on his journey of discovery. But it's unfamiliar territory and failure is not an option. He seeks out small business leaders to help, but he's unsure how to reach them or talk to them when he finds them. There's so much work to be done, and the weather is changing. Thunderclaps of rising inflation spell recession storms on the way. Whole communities struggle with the rising tides of cost of living, whilst they try and clear up the debris left by the pandemic. A reduced labour market, pressure to be net-zero, uncertainty on when the sun will rise again in Europe. It's almost too much to bear.

But then, just for a moment, the clouds clear. From within their shelters, communities of small business owners emerge ready to fight – if only someone could teach them how. Michael knows he cannot do this alone. He needs someone that can bring courage, intelligence and heart, capable of getting the things done he needs to do his job and help his small business customers.

"I'll help you," said a confident woman sounding like she knew what she was talking about. "We'll help you," echoed a sea of voices behind her.

"Small business owners, we know you. We hear you. We understand. Life's tough at the moment, but there are people out there that have ridden this storm before. And they're ready to lead you to safety. Because together we can get through this and come out stronger, ready to face whatever gets thrown at us next."

"Michael, with your resources and our experience, immense data and insight and tenacity, we can make a difference, and you can trust us to make it happen. We'll face things no-one's had to tackle before, and we might get things wrong, but that's OK. Because when we work together, we're ready for anything. Now let's get a plan together for you."

Our hero took the plan to the Powers That Be with a renewed sense of optimism. Finally, a way forward for the small business owners to get the support they need. But wait. A problem. The Powers That Be didn't 'get it.' They were suspicious of the people Michael had met that day of the storm. Who are they? What right do they have to play? Why should we give them our riches to help others? Luckily for Michael, the people he'd met 'got it.' They'd faced similar cynicism in the past and were well used to having to sell their ideas. Working collaboratively with Michael, they built the business case and grew legitimacy through sharing their knowledge and insight. They weren't afraid to experiment either, knowing that it still moves you forward when something doesn't work.

Michael was relieved knowing he had a plan to deliver, and he was excited to make an impact. He felt like there was finally a break in the storm, time to breathe, but safe in the knowledge he had the resilience now to deal with future uncertainty. He knew now that no matter what happened next, he had people he could trust, willing to take on the shared responsibility of delivering positive change and increasing his ability to understand and help small business leaders better.

Reflecting on his journey, Michael made one final realisation. In achieving this important mission, he'd been able to fulfil his ambitions and had a new sense of happiness based not just on the recognition from his team and peers but from knowing he had done something that mattered for the greater good. Michael was home.

If you're ready and willing to invest in new ways to help your small business customers be more productive, and want to associate yourself with a positive mission that also speaks to your own needs, come speak to us. We'll help you find home.

Fun huh? It certainly went down a storm with the sales team when I helped them understand how the main themes from the story could help them hit their targets!

Time to Work on the Details

You've figured out why you're telling your story and you have an idea about what type of story you want it to be. Now it's time to brainstorm the who, what, where, when and why.

WHO IS YOUR STORY ABOUT?

It's easier for your audience to connect with a single specific person than a vague group, so start by figuring out who your main character is. Focus your story on their experiences – experiences that you know your audience are likely to share, so they can identify with the character and cheer for them as the story unfolds. Your main character could be a real person, could be fictional, it could even be an object but remember – it's never you.

Give them a name and think about what they are like. What scares them? What keeps them up at night? What stops them achieving what they are trying to do? What excites them? What makes them feel happy, fulfilled, in charge, important? What do they value? And what behaviours can't they stand? What is their shared experience or view of the world that aligns to your own? Maybe they're starting up a business just like you, trying to find meaning in their life or just wanting to adorn their homes with pretty objects (just like you). Whatever it is – it doesn't always have to be big and meaningful to everyone – just to you and your ideal client is enough.

WHAT HAPPENS IN YOUR STORY?

Thinking only about your main character, what is the problem they face? What's happened to them to make them need to solve it now? What barriers are getting in their way? How might you be able to help them overcome those sticking points? This is a great time to introduce yourself as someone that helped to show them the way. Think specifically about how you and your products did this.

WHEN AND WHERE DOES YOUR STORY HAPPEN?

Adding a few specific details – when your story happened, where, what the weather was like etc helps your audience paint a mental picture and makes it more likely for them to connect personally with it. Think about what relevant details you can add in to bring your words to life (but keep it brief – like little titbits to fire up someone's brain but without overloading them with lots of unnecessary and unhelpful waffle).

Here is an example of this in action in a story I helped create for maker Belinda Knott, the founder of Pothies and inventor of the viral Cosymajig, a wearable hot water bottle carrier.

> ### A chilly realisation
>
> Fast forward to January 2019 and my first-time chill, swimming in the sea off Wales. As I watched others stuffing hot water bottles down their trousers to warm up and felt the pain of my

defrosting hands, inspiration struck! A hot water bottle sling WITH pockets!

WHY DID YOUR STORY HAPPEN?

When we explore story structure later on in this chapter, we'll look at the idea of 'inciting incidents.' This is basically something that happened to someone that made the next step they had to take inevitable. Like being made redundant. Think about what was happening to your main character even before they met you or found your products or services. Was something making them unhappy? Were they struggling to get the help they needed? Were they at a crossroads? Were they forced into a seemingly losing situation? Did meeting you show them the possibilities of a new way, or change their outlook?

SECTION 2 – HOW TO GET YOUR STORIES SIZZLING

"Put in more WOW words. We don't have enough WOW words. WOW WORDS NOW!" For some reason, I feel compelled to say that in a demanding Anna Delvey 'Inventing Anna' voice but in reality, it came from a brand and comms manager at BT, a client of the old marketing agency I used to run.

We were getting ripped into; the copy I'd written wasn't exciting enough, it needed more … you guessed it … wow. But are words really all that are needed to turn a dull story into a compelling one? Well, you're about to find out.

Hopefully by now, you've got the bare bones of your story (substance). Now it's time to turn it into something dramatic, exciting, memorable and most importantly, it gets your audience to do what you need them to do next.

Unlike my BT WOW words man, I think it takes a bit more than just a few interesting words sprinkled around to make a good story. For me, it's all about emotion. And the connection this emotion creates between your audience and you.

There are three questions I'd like you to consider:

1. What do you want your ideal client to feel when they read your story?

- A sense of achievement
- Ambition
- Belonging
- Being seen and heard
- Joyful
- In control
- Optimistic about the future
- Hopeful that anything is possible

2. What is the problem you are solving for your ideal client by telling this story?

- What isn't working for them right now?
- What can't they avoid any longer?
- What are they trying to fix and why can't they do it already?

- Why are you best placed to help?
- What can you help them do that they couldn't do without you?

3. What wisdom do you provide through your story?

- What realisation did your main character have after meeting you?
- How do your own experiences qualify you to help guide them?
- How did you share your wisdom and help them achieve success, whatever that looked like for them?
- What did the relationship between you and your main character look and feel like for them? What was the experience of buying from you like?
- What is life like for them now?
- What have you learned from the experience which you can take forward to help others in the future?

Figuring these three areas out will really help make sure every story you write sparkles. Once you're confident in writing, there are a few other creative hacks you might want to try.

Life is an Emotional Rollercoaster
Tips for adding tension and delivering impact

It's a bright summer's day. A young girl is enjoying an ice cream by the sea. Sticky strawberry sauce is dripping down the cone onto her tiny hands. Her massive grins tells you how much she's enjoying it. How does that make you feel? Happy? Hungry? Now imagine a greedy seagull, torpedoing down and snatching the ice cream, causing the girl to sob big, messy tears. How quickly does your mood change?

The most compelling stories swing between negative and positive emotions. This helps create a sense of conflict, excitement, satisfaction and resolution, and prevents the audience from nodding off halfway through.

Take my happy summer scene for example. The mental picture of the girl made us feel good for sure, but we're not on the edge of our seats. As far as we know, she'll finish her snack, head on home and live happily ever after. Or not. But it's likely we wouldn't stick around long enough to find out.

Enter the evil seagull. All of a sudden, there's chaos. The illusion is smashed. What's going to happen to the girl we wonder? Will her parents berate her for her lack of attention? Could this be a trigger for a big adventure where they seek to banish all seagulls from the land, or will they just go buy her another ice cream? Whatever happens next, we know we want to stick around to find out.

Have a think about your own story and the stories of those you help. How can you use emotion to keep people interested? Maybe using more descriptive, emotive words to move your content away from facts and figures to feelings. In my ice cream example, I talked about the size of the girl's smile and included that is was a sunny day, all words which help us create that happy mental picture.

Can you add some drama by swinging your narrative between negative and positive? It doesn't have to be life or death – maybe something as simple as a customer had a problem, it was making them really unhappy, they find a solution (or at least they thought they did) but then it failed, leaving them in an even worse place, until they found you.

This is something called a false summit. It's like climbing a hill, thinking you're near the top and then up pops the real summit from under the cloud. You'll have experienced this yourself, probably when watching a film or drama. The problem's been building, you think the protagonist is about to solve it and live happily ever after and then BOOM, something else comes along that they have to overcome. Adding a false summit to your story is a great way to keep people hooked for longer – and make sure they're really rooting for your main character. Describe some of the challenges they faced along the way, setbacks you faced together, moments of wobble, tears, frustration. But don't forget the happy ending. Or, if you can't do happy, at least make sure there's resolution. There's nothing more frustrating than a story that goes nowhere.

Remember – not every story needs to finish on a cliff hanger but a little bit of up and down will help keep your reader's interest and leave them wanting more.

And finally, don't forget humour. Used well, it lifts a story and often can really humanise an otherwise tricky subject. Just don't forget to think about your audience and what would be appropriate to them!

Where Do You Draw the Line Between Fact and Fiction When Telling Your Story?

In 1942, archaeologist, Flinders Petrie, died whilst living in Jerusalem. He donated his head to the Royal College of Surgeons in London, which his wife carried back to the UK in a hat box. It was then promptly lost, due to the war, and found many years later in a cupboard. Or so the story went.

When I was a child, my grandparents rented their house from an old school friend of Grandpa's, an artist called Anne Petrie. Flinders Petrie was her father, and my siblings and I grew up hearing lots about him. As I'm sure you can imagine, I was fascinated by the idea of the hat box and the lost head. The problem is, it's not 100% true. Losing the head, yep, that happened, but sadly, the hat box is purely a work of fiction. Thanks for bursting my bubble Wikipedia.

But you know what? It doesn't stop me from telling this story over and over again. It's a great icebreaker when meeting new people at parties, and I swear it's what landed me a project for audit firm KPMG – but that's another tale altogether.

So where do you draw the line between fact and fiction? When does applying a bit of creative license turn into defrauding your audience? And does it matter?

In a word yes, it really does matter.

Adding dramatic details to your stories, maybe changing the setting slightly to create more intrigue, is all part of painting a more engaging picture for your audience. As is creating an imaginary scenario to help your customers see what working with you or using your product could look and feel like for them. Providing it's clear it's fictional, this can be a powerful way to bring what you do to life, especially if your business is relatively new and you haven't yet sold anything.

But making something up and presenting it as real – that's a different matter. As is taking someone else's work or words and passing them off as yours.

One of the key reasons I advocate storytelling in business is its ability to create bonds and build trust between you and your audience, people who will potentially buy from you. Without that trust, selling to them will be much harder, if not impossible. Break that trust part way through the relationship, for example, by telling a lie, and you can kiss that customer goodbye, but probably not before they've gone and told 10 other potential customers of yours what you've done.

And don't fall into the trap of saying things that aren't true because you see other people doing it. Values are often where I see this happen. For example, a shoe company claiming to be ethical and sustainable whose suppliers use child labour. Or an authentic Italian restaurant that nips to the supermarket for their pizza dough (both of which I've personally experienced).

If you spin a little yarn to make an already memorable story stick in your audience's head (just like my story – excuse the pun! That's one thing. But making something up entirely and passing it off as the truth? It's just not worth it.

What About Fear? Good storytelling technique or plain old scaremongering?

Business owners who don't tell their story are 92% more likely to fail in the first 2 years of trading.

Attention-grabbing maybe. But does this approach say the right thing about my brand?

Before you start panicking, that stat is entirely made up. I've got no idea of how likely your business is to succeed, storytelling or not.

I do know that as a founder myself, sharing my story has really helped me build an engaged audience and create solid connections, many of which have converted to sales. And experience shows me that this success has been replicated across almost every business I've worked with. But still, I'm not going to start telling people that if you don't do it, you're failing. As well as being inaccurate, it goes completely against my values, and I'm sure, as anything, it wouldn't align with your values either.

Fear is a potent emotion and, as such, should be used wisely. Scaremongering, clickbait, and trying to frighten your audience into doing something send an unmistakable message about who you are and what your brand stands for. I'm guessing that most of you, if not all of you, don't want to be seen like that.

Here's an alternative approach which sends all the right vibes:

1. Take the time to understand what your customers are afraid of and dig beyond the surface. For example, many of the people I work with will tell me they don't have the time to think about their story when really what they mean is they're too scared to think about their story because that would mean they have to tell it publicly and they fear being judged or laughed at.

2. Turn those fears on their head. Turn a negative into a positive by showing your clients an alternative reality where they no longer have that fear and what life could look like for them then. Make sure you show how you could help them make that a reality.

3. Share stories of where you've overcome similar fears and what you went on to do as a result. Even better, share stories of how you've helped others do that through your work or the products you sell.

An Analogy, Metaphor and Simile Walk into a Business Story...

If you're a parent, or regularly look after youngsters, you'll understand the pain of your little darling coming home from school and asking you to explain the difference between a pronoun and adverb. Don't even get me started on conjunctions and interjections. And that's coming from a writer! So whilst I'm not suggesting you go dig out your old GCSE text books, there are a few little tricks of the English language that can add a touch of spice, creativity and more importantly clarity to your stories, making them even more engaging and memorable.

Metaphors, analogies and similes are a handy technique for stories where you want to show more than you tell (which should be pretty much all the time). Note – 'Show, don't tell' is a clever technique storytellers use to make readers feel they're part of the story. So rather than telling them what's happening in a factual way, 'showing' eg through their actions or words, introduces details and creates nuances to get a deeper meaning across. Think 'life is like a box of chocolates,' 'she's a shining star,' or 'it was as cold as ice.'

Analogies:

Imagine you're explaining a complex business concept to someone who's not familiar with what you do – that's where a good analogy can come in handy. I apply this all the time when trying to explain to my mum what exactly it is I do for a living … it's not frustrating in the slightest that after all these years, she still doesn't quite 'get it.' Hmmpf.

Analogies are a way of painting vivid pictures that help your ideal clients understand unfamiliar ideas by comparing them to something far more relatable. They establish connections and bridge gaps in knowledge, making sure your stories are more accessible to all. For example, "Pitching a storytelling book is like riding a rollercoaster. It makes you want to vomit with fear at times but it's worth the exhilarating ride."

Metaphors:

Metaphors are powerful tools that infuse your business stories with symbolism, depth and imagery. They create a direct comparison between two unrelated things, highlighting shared characteristics. Metaphors evoke emotions, spark imagination and leave a lasting, memorable impression. For instance, "My coaching course is a lighthouse, guiding customers through the stormy seas of life and providing a beacon of trust and support." Ok, so that might be a little bit on the cheesy side, but hopefully you get what I mean.

Similes:

If you love making comparisons using 'like' or 'as' then similes are going to be your go-to friends. Similes are a bit like metaphors but they use explicit comparison words to draw connections between two dissimilar things. Confused? Here's an example: "Her negotiation skills were as sharp as a double-edged sword, cutting through any obstacles in her path. Similes are great for adding colour and playfulness to your stories, making them more relatable and engaging.

Word to the wise. All these techniques are great but just remember to use them sparingly ensuring they serve your purpose and enhance understanding, rather than overshadowing the core message you are wanting to communicate.

SECTION 3 – FROM INTRODUCTION TO EPIC ENDING

How you can use the Three Act Structure to write better stories

If I were to tell you that a story has a beginning, middle and end, would you want your money back?

OK, so maybe I'm simplifying things just a little, but truthfully, the way we were taught to construct a story at school, is exactly the way all stories are constructed. It doesn't mean you have to always tell them in a linear form. TV shows love to start at the end and tell stories backwards – *Daisy Jones and the Six* on Amazon Prime is a perfect example of this … and oh so good; the clothes, the music, the passion, Sam Claflin's hair … sorry, I got lost there for a moment, where was I?

Oh yeah structure.

The Three Act Structure (beginning, middle and end or crisis, struggle and resolution) is nothing new. It's the basis of stories throughout time, dating all the way back to Aristotle (fancy, huh?). Storytelling big wigs like John Yorke and Robert McKee believe that if you compare all successful stories, they always have one thing in common – structure. And I would tend to agree with this. But, as I've said before, be careful not to confuse plot or story for structure.

If you've already worked on your Substance and Sizzle, this next piece should be an exercise in pulling everything together. You shouldn't be adding anything new to your story, as you've already figured out your characters, the question you're answering for them and the plot line.

Structure is just about finding the right home for all your thoughts.

Act 1. The beginning

This is where you want to be setting the scene and adding context for your story (the who, what, where, why and when stuff). Introduce your main character, talk about the problem they're looking to solve (their CRISIS) and the inciting incident that led to this, and build some suspense. Are they going to find a solution or is it going to end badly for them?

Act 2. The middle

This is where your sparkle comes in. Talk about the emotional ups and downs your main character experienced (their STRUGGLE). You could even throw in a false summit to increase the drama. This is when your audience feels like the story is about to be resolved but then it's snatched away. *Four Weddings and a Funeral* is a good example of this – you think Hugh Grant's Charles and Andie McDowell's Carrie finally get together … only for Carrie to reveal she is engaged to someone else! Arghh (don't worry, they end up together in the end – is it raining? I hadn't noticed…). The middle section is also where you can introduce yourself as the clever one, sharing your wisdom and showing how you supported your customer. Think Gandalf in *Lord of the Rings*.

Act 3. The end

There is nothing more frustrating than an unresolved story, so don't forget to talk about the solution and most importantly, the impact that had on your customer (RESO-LUTION). What is life like for them now they've solved their problem? What are they able to do that they couldn't before? You might also want to include some of your own personal reflections at this stage. What did this experience teach you? What did you learn that you can now take forward with other customers that have similar problems?

And then, and this is the biggie, think about what you want your key takeaway and call to action to be. There is zero point in getting this far, only to forget your call to action and have your audience unsure of where they need to go next or what you want them to do.

Make. It. Clear.

You don't need to make it overly cheesy, just a clear signpost for anyone who has identified themselves in your story, shares a similar problem to your protagonist and wants to know what they have to do to feel like your customer, after buying from or working with you.

For the business stories I tell, this might be something like:

"If you see an easier future when you're free from worrying about judgement every time you tell your story, just like Jennifer does, let's chat."

What's in a Headline? Umm… Everything!

*"To hook us, what happens next must bring with it
a consequence that makes a difference."*

Lisa Cron

I'm going to say this straight. You can write the world's greatest story but without a compelling hook upfront, it's likely that no-one will ever read it. So stop leaving all the great stuff to the end of your story, hoping it will make people read on. It won't. They'll never get there to find it. Harsh, I know, but totes true. It wasn't always that way, but with attention spans like gnats and a whole hairy heap of content thrown our way every single second of the day, as storytellers, we have to work über hard now to grab the interest of our ideal clients. A good headline will do this for you, telling your reader everything they need to know at a high level before they move on. A great headline will leave them no choice in wanting to read on for all the juicy details. And of course, an awesome call to action will make them take action and, dear reader, your job will be done.

Here are my top tips for grabbing attention with your story headlines (along with some real examples I've used in my own content):

Spell out what's in it for your audience. Stop trying to be clever. Tell your reader exactly what you want them to know and do and don't worry that you're giving all the good stuff away upfront. This is what our brains want/need. If your audience is interested after the first hook – and most importantly it's clear what's in it for them, they will read on.

Example headline: *"How ditching the glitz in favour of honest storytelling can help you build trust. My top three tips."*

Get emotional. There's a lot of data around that suggest emotional content increases effectiveness. Even adding emojis makes a difference with some brands reporting up to 56% increase in email open rates when they've use them. Bonkers right? Using emotion creates an instant grab, triggering something in your audience's brain that subconsciously informs them they'd be better off if they read what you have to say.

Example headline: *"I cried in Pret a Manger and it taught me an important lesson."*

Be bold (but don't forget the payoff): How does the saying go? 'Curiosity got the cat to open your email?' That's right yeah? Asking leading questions in your content headlines, posing an intriguing hypothesis or promising your audience something so audacious they simply have to read on is a great way to hook people in. But don't forget to give them the answers in the first sentence or so. There's no point in coming up with a great question in your headline if you waffle on for the first three paragraphs before finally answering it or, worse still, never answer it.

Example headline (and payoff): *"If someone offered to create free content you could use time and time again to boost sales, what would you say? Customer success stories are exactly that,* *ready-made content for you to share with your audience at no extra cost."*

I'm going to be a little bit humble now and tell you that it's taken me years of practice to get this stuff right, so please don't beat yourself up if it's feeling a bit hard right now. No-one expects you to read this book and be an expert straightaway – and neither do you need to be. It's all about building the muscles, trying something new, getting feedback, adapting and learning what your audience like and don't like, day by day. With that in mind, here are some of the things I've learnt over the years writing stories – and a few of the mistakes I've made, so you don't have you!

No. 1 A mistake I've definitely been guilty of is making my story all about me. It's never about you. Even when it's your 'About Me' story. Confusing right? Not really. Stories, even those about our own experiences are always about the person you are trying to connect with. In business terms that means your ideal client. Put them, their needs, their problem at the heart of every story you tell and you won't go far wrong.

No. 2 Don't leave all the good stuff to the end of your story. In fact, bring it right up front in your headline to hook people in. Leading with your clever insight, big realisation or special offer gives your readers an incentive to want to learn more. No incentive – they won't stick around long enough to get to the bottom.

And finally – don't, I mean DON'T forget your call to action. A story that goes nowhere is a wasted effort. Make sure you tell your audience what to do next if your story has inspired them and how they can get involved.

So there are my slip ups to avoid but what about some wisdom?

When you're writing your story, stick the following words on a post-it note next to your desk; emotion, impact, connection and action to remind you of the following:

1. **EMOTION:** Your audience don't want to know what happened but how it felt, leaving them asking the question, "What do I have to do to feel like that too?" Make sure you include emotional and sensory words like, "Mary felt scared but excited about the prospect for change..." or "George was so close to success, he could almost taste it."

2. **IMPACT:** You want your audience to be thinking, "How could working with you or buying your products change their life like the person in your story? So don't leave out the juicy stuff – how you made a mark, what change you initiated in your main character, what life was like for them as a result.

3. **CONNECTION:** A story told well to the right audience should be like holding up a mirror to them, leaving them thinking, "I'm experiencing exactly the same as the person in this story – it must be for me?" So make sure you don't just talk about the end result but the reason your character needed you in the first place.

4. **ACTION:** I've said it before (literally, just now) and I'll keep on saying it. Don't waste a good story by not telling your audience what to do next. You want them to end your story with one positive thought, "I'm ready to feel like the person in this story. Where do I sign up?"

Some Final Thoughts: How do you want your words to feel?

Despite making a career out of being a writer and storyteller, I often get my words wrong.

"I'm tolerable," I told my partner Tim the other day describing my flexibility towards an annoying situation.

"Don't you mean tolerant?"

"Dammit. I've done it again haven't !?"

Thankfully for my paying clients, I'm fine when writing. It's just when I'm chatting away. A malaprop if you will (is that even the right word? Or is it a spoonerism?). You'd never know I had an English A-Level.

Tim tells me it's adorable (I'm not sure about that), but one thing I do know is that I never lose sleep over it. Neither do I lie awake at night worrying about the limitations of my vocabulary or my sometimes shoddy spelling, especially in Instagram posts.

Going about my day, telling my story, I worry less about the words I use, and more about how they make others feel. Long fancy words are not my thing – but more importantly they're not right for my audience either. I'm all about simplifying and demystifying storytelling, so how would it benefit me to write or speak in a way that was hard to understand, un-relatable or worse still, gave an air of elitism; like I was in some way superior to you? That's really not my vibe and I bet if it was, you wouldn't be here now.

I want you to feel inspired by my words but in a way that's achievable, not a distant unreachable goal.

I want you to feel comforted, part of something great, safe, joyful, excited about what a future of telling your story could hold.

And that's what I use my words for. Not bamboozling you or trying to prove my superiority as a writer.

So, if you set about writing your stories and you find yourself reaching for the thesaurus for the fanciest pantciest words you can find. Don't.

Stop and think first about your audience. How do you want your words to make them feel?

Write like you speak. Read your text out loud and if you stumble over any weird words you wouldn't normally use, take them out until it feels natural again.

And finally, don't just write what you know, write what you know **emotionally**. Use stories to express your experiences, your feelings, and bring people in closer to the words you're sharing.

Just a little caveat – there are times when a more formal writing approach is needed. For example, academic or technical writing, but again, it comes down to one thing really – who your audience is and what they will relate most to. And, of course, let's not forget your authentic voice too. If you are a wordy and that works for your audience, then go forth my confederate (go for it my friend).

THE GOOD STUFF TO REMEMBER

Before you get started, get clear on the purpose of your story and the type of narrative you want to convey. It might help to think about it in terms of a crisis (problem), a struggle (what was done to try and fix it) and a resolution (the solution and the impact). And don't forget the internal transformation of your lead character (you or your dream client) is key here.

Make it easy on yourself by using classic plot structures like Rags to Riches (think Cinderella) or Voyage and Return, and align them with your story's purpose. Remember to focus on substance over style, knowing why you're telling your story and how it connects with the experiences, problems and values of your dream client, rather than getting caught up in fancy words and techniques. By getting clear on purpose and structure, you'll create a solid foundation for telling engaging and impactful stories.

Your headline is essential to capture the attention of your audience and draw them in to your story. It should clearly communicate what's in it for them, evoke an emotion like intrigue and be bold yet also deliver an obvious call to action. Personally, I find writing the headline at the end the easiest approach, once I know exactly what my story is trying to say and why.

Ultimately, prioritise authenticity (real experiences in yours or your customer's voice) and simplicity to ensure your dream clients feel inspired, comforted and connected through your stories.

CHAPTER 6
ENGAGE: HOW TO CREATE
STORY-LED CONTENT

DISCOVERING STORIES IN YOUR EVERYDAY TO CONNECT YOU WITH YOUR DREAM CLIENT

Three years ago, I found myself telling a bunch of corporate sales people during a training session about how I used to write little books held together with wonky staples when I was a child. As the words left my mouth, I remember thinking, how did I get here? This wasn't what they came to hear. Surely I should be sharing some grand story showcasing my successes? But no, instead, I'm basically back in primary school, doing a show and tell.

But you know what. It worked. The audience didn't know me from Adam (or Eve for that matter). They didn't care about my CV. But they did want to learn to be better storytellers (to help them sell more and get richer). What better person to teach them than someone who had been telling stories from the moment they could write.

Here's the lesson: we can all tell predictable stories about our business but unfortunately (and check LinkedIn for evidence of this) when you've heard one, you've heard them all. To be really good business storytellers, you need to be looking under the surface, away from the obvious stories, to the more interesting and insightful angles that will not only help you stand apart from the crowd but that will really help your customers understand why you or your products/services are the best option for them.

But before we get into this, I need to get something off my chest. Wanna know what really gets my goat? (And if this is you, I mean no offence). People that tell me they have no stories to tell. Stories are literally everywhere, you just need to know where to look.

In the words of Dostoevsky (get me and my fancy literary references!), "How could you live and have no story to tell?"

Stories exist within every single one of us and we don't have to be literary geniuses to tell them. You've probably already told several stories today, without even realising it.

But when it comes to intentional storytelling for our businesses, it's not uncommon to be totally lost for inspiration. Firstly, I would say, a lot of this comes from the pressure we put on ourselves to come up with Pulitzer Prize worthy stories (there really is goodness to be found in the everyday). And secondly the minute we pick up a pen or open a new document, we doubt our abilities to have any stories inside us.

Just think for a minute about the last time you met a friend for a drink and they asked, "How's life?" The chances are rather than just saying 'fine' or 'rubbish,' you spent the time telling them a story about your week, the ups and downs, twists and turns. Without knowing it, your seemingly mundane reflection will have likely included drama, suspense, humour – even if it was just a tale about your dog getting sick or a strange encounter on the bus.

And whilst I'm busting some myths, here's another. Storytelling is not just for service-led businesses. Some of the very best business storytellers are product brands who either use story to bring their products to life, giving them their own voices and identities or who do a great job of capturing the stories of those who use their products.

One of my favourite projects I've worked on was for luxury bag brand, Gladstn London. When founder, Richard Sharman, (one of my few male clients) got in touch all he had was an idea and a very blank sheet of paper. So I chanced my luck. And proposed a rather different approach not normally associated with high-end products; I created characters for the bags. Now I'm not talking Percy Pig, Colin Caterpillar cartoons (but way-to-go M&S with your storytelling!) But instead, I built distinct personalities for each of the brand's bags, based on how customers were likely to use them and the journeys they would take with them. The tone of voice was genteel yet adventurous, very much in line with Gladstn's target customer base.

Take their weekend bag, for example, which I had great fun naming Late Nights and Lie Ins.

"I'm not work, I'm play. I'm a wandering star. An escapist. A romantic. I dream of spontaneous adventures."

Or Freedom of the City, a multi-purpose bag launched just as the world was re-awakening, post Covid lockdowns.

"I'm a celebration of life. A fresh start, a new adventure, a re-kindling of old flames. I'm freedom. Sitting by your side wherever your everyday journey takes you. I'm the treat you deserve as you step back into the light, re-connecting with the people and places you love once more."

These are serious products that come with a serious price tag but that doesn't mean you can't inject some personality and life. Plus in a high-end fashion world full of stuffy designers, this story-led approach was exactly what Gladstn London needed to differentiate themselves from the get-go.

Hunting High and Low: Find hidden business story gems in your everyday.

I think it's safe to say by now we've fully established that you are, in fact, already a storyteller. You just need to find the right stories to tell. Plot spoiler – they're everywhere.

Stories are in your personal journey, how you set up your business, and the mission you're on now. They're in the experiences of your customers working with you and how you've impacted their life. Stories are in the people you work with, your teams, those you collaborate with, your community or tribe. And they're in the world around you; the things you see and feel, your sense of purpose, your desire to change and make a difference, the causes you follow and the beliefs you hold.

SOMETHING TO THINK ABOUT:

Using the guide below, have a think about where you could look for stories. Don't worry about the end result at this stage, just bullet or mind map whatever jumps into your head.

Things that have happened to me

- Go back to the beginning. What was the moment you realised your calling? What obstacles have you had to overcome to get to where you are now?
- Talk about a time you smashed it. And a time you didn't.
- Share who and what inspires you and how this impacts how you help others.
- Talk about how a happy customer makes you feel.

Stories about my customers and other people I work with

- Invite your customers to tell your story for you.
- Celebrate your customers' success.
- Show how you've helped others experience

new things.

- Talk about the communities you are part of and how they help you do what you do.

Stories about my products or services

- Give your products a voice and a story – get creative!
- Share the story of how you developed what you do, where you source from, the people you've met along the way etc.
- Use stories to show rather than tell your ideal clients about the benefits of what you do or sell.
- Create fictional scenarios to help others see how their world would look in the future if they were to engage with you and what you do.

Stories about my social purpose or a cause I believe in

- Talk about the bigger picture of why you do what you do.
- Evidence your higher purpose. Why is it so important to you?
- How does your purpose fit into your vision and how would you like others to fit into that?

Great. You've got a tonne of story ideas. So what? Do you just go out and tell them all at once? No, of course not, that would be bonkers. This is where your marketing strategy comes in, aligning what stage you're at with your business and the specific goals you have with the stories that will support you best in achieving them.

The stories you share when first launching your business will be different from when you're more established and have a new product or service to sell. Here are some examples to help you.

LAUNCHING YOUR BUSINESS

Story ideas

- **Share your founder or origin story to help your new audience connect with you:** Why did you start your business? What problem were you trying to solve?

- **Highlight personal motivation:** What inspired you? What challenges did you overcome?

- **Showcase early supporters:** Who helped you along the way? How did they contribute?

Template

Hook: Start with a compelling anecdote or moment that sparked the idea for your business.

Background: Explain the context and challenges that led to the decision to start your business. Include some interesting or unexpected details if you can; and don't forget to share the emotional side – how did all this feel for you?

Transformational path: Describe the steps you took to turn your idea into reality, including key milestones and setbacks. Make it realistic, not picture perfect, to build trust.

Resolution: Finish by shining a light on your business right now, how you feel as you launch it and where you want to go with it in the future (your vision). Add details to show your audience what they can expect and how this is going to impact them and help solve the problem they have.

SELLING A NEW PRODUCT OR SERVICE

Story ideas

- **Use customer stories:** Share testimonials or success stories from guinea pig customers or early adopters. If you don't have any of these, why not create fictional scenarios of the impact it could have on a specific customer.

- **Demonstrate the need you're addressing:** Showcase your understanding and expertise by explain the problem your new product/service solves and why it matters to your dream clients.

- **Behind-the-scenes:** Everyone loves a good nosey! Show how you developed your product or service, including trials, errors, and breakthroughs.

Template

Hook: Introduce the problem with a relatable scenario or question.

Problem: Describe the issue in detail, emphasising its impact on your dream clients from both a practical and emotional perspective. For example, being fearful of sharing your story means that new customers won't know about you (practical) but also can leave you feeling frustrated and questioning your self-worth (emotional).

Solution: Introduce your new product or service and show how it addresses the problem. Create scenarios and characters to bring this to life rather than just telling people about it. Think about the medium that you use – could be video, like Reels or a TikTok, be a quick and easy way of showcasing what's new and how to use it?

Proof: Share testimonials, case studies, or user-generated content (social media posts that your customers have created and shared). Why not interview a customer on an Instagram Live, invite them onto your podcast or ask them to write a guest blog for your website?

Call to Action: Be very specific about how your dream clients can try your new product or service; make it really easy for them eg online signup, buy now button etc. If appropriate, encourage with a special offer or incentive.

Story ideas

- **Success stories:** Highlight how your course has helped previous attendees – what transformation did they go through? What can they do now that they couldn't before? Even better, get a past student to tell this story for you!

- **Your personal background:** Share your story as the course creator and how your experiences and expertise, that feed into the content, can help your dream clients.

- **Preview content:** Give a sneak peek of what attendees will learn, to entice them in and spark some FOMO.

Template

Hook: Start with an inspiring story or statistic related to your course.

Problem: Explain the common issue your course addresses – again dig deep with this and think about both the obvious problem and how this might be impacting people emotionally.

Solution: Introduce your course and what people will learn and gain from attending.

Proof: Share testimonials or success stories.

Call to Action: Encourage sign-ups with a sense of urgency – this could be an early-bird offer or limited places. Think about creating a wait list to build excitement.

To help get your creative juices flowing, here are some other ideas for stories you may not have thought about that you can build into your ongoing marketing and content plans.

THE COMMUNITY IMPACT STORY

This is an opportunity for you to share how your small business has positively influenced your community. Maybe you've partnered with local charities, organised awesome community events, implemented sustainable practices or just spoken at your child's school careers day. By showcasing your community involvement, you are demonstrating your commitment to social responsibility and showing your ideal clients that you're not just here to make a profit, but to make a difference, something which they will be able to connect to in their own lives.

Talk about: What's important to you and what you believe in. Give specific examples of things you've done, how you've developed products or services in response to an environmental or social issue in your community. Talk about people you've worked with and causes that you've championed that demonstrate your values and ethics.

Share what this means to your customers or even how they can get involved to create a sense of unity and momentum.

THE BEHIND-THE-SCENES STORY

This is one of my favourites, where you pull back the curtain to give your ideal clients a sneak peek into the daily operations and the hard work that goes into running your businesses. It's those interesting anecdotes, challenges you've overcome, and unique ways of working that set you apart. By sharing this personal side of your businesses, you help our audience connect with you on a more human level.

Talk about: How and where you work, where you get your inspiration, how you create something, where you source materials, who else is in your office (even your pets count!)

YOUR FOUNDER STORY (AKA – THE ABOUT ME STORY)

Don't overlook this one, thinking you can only tell it once. Your story is always special because it's your unique journey. It's a chance to delve into what inspired you to start your small businesses, the challenges you faced, and those pivotal moments that shaped who you are now and the value you provide. This story is a great way to humanise your brand and gives your audience a deeper understanding of the passion and vision behind what you do. It's a chance to show them that you're more than just a business owner – you're a dreamer and a doer!

Talk about: why you started your business; the problem you were trying to fix; what you were doing when the inspiration hit you; what challenges you had to overcome along the way and how this helps you better understand and empathise with what your customers want/need, the origins of your brand name etc.

THE FAILURES AND LESSONS LEARNED STORY

We've all faced setbacks, made mistakes, and encountered challenges along the way. But guess what? These stories can be incredibly inspiring and insightful. By openly acknowledging your failures and discussing the lessons you've learned, you demonstrate resilience, adaptability, and a commitment to continuous improvement. And hey, it's a great chance for your audience to learn from your experiences too!

Talk about: a time when something didn't go your way; how it made you feel and react; how it impacted you in the moment; how you moved on from the setback; what you took away from the experience and how this helps you now; the way you run your business and how you support your clients.

THE TRANSFORMATION STORY

Give your customer (real or fictional) main character energy and tell a story that shows their transformation as they work with you or use your products. It's a great way to create a little bit of FOMO, making your customers feel they want to experience the same) whilst shoe-horning in product or service benefits and features without it being dull or feeling like a sales pitch.

Talk about: what they're trying to achieve (their dreams, ambitions, the problem they need solving), what happens when they meet you; how you show empathy and understanding, how you, your product or service help them solve their problem, what you help them avoid, and what success looks like for them after buying from you.

TOP TIPS: WHAT TO DO WHEN YOUR CREATIVE JUICES RUN DRY

I love to keep a repository of story ideas for those days when you're staring down a blank sheet of paper. This could be a notebook, Trello board, carved into a rock, whatever works for you. Just something you can easily add thoughts to, as and when they come to you. Something funny happens, write it down. A client gives you a piece of wisdom, make note of it. You feel a certain way about something you see in the press, scribble it down. Even if you're not quite sure what purpose they serve, or you can't see how they would make story or piece of content, just jot them down continually so, when you're having a slow creative day, you at the very least have a lovely list of prompts to get you started.

Get your audience to help you out. Use a poll on Instagram to find out what your followers would like to hear you talk about. Run a Mailchimp survey for your newsletter subscribers. Ask your customers directly. Not only is it a great way to generate ideas, it's great for building relationships. Who doesn't like to be asked their opinion?

Come back to your brand story. If you've been listening for a while, you'll have heard me talk about your brand story being the foundations of every story you tell. That said, you can't talk every day about your purpose, vision, mission and values. But, if you haven't mentioned it in a while and are in need of story-led content ideas, why not revisit and share elements of it with your audience. Don't forget to tell them why it should matter to them – for example, why your values help them get the best experience from working with you.

Turn to your customers for ideas. What stories can you tell about people you've worked with recently? Can you turn a product testimonial into a short story, adding your own unique insights? What about sharing an experience of how you helped someone? Or even a story about how you met – did they stalk you on Insta, did you meet in person, were you referred, did they have a funny reason for needing what you make or sell?

Re-purpose for the win. Just because you've already told a story once doesn't mean you can't tell it again. Take a look back at old content. What stories can you re-purpose?

- Use Instagram stories and Reels to engage your audience with captivating visual storytelling. It could be something as simple as photos from the workshop you ran for your customer, some cool before and after shots of the house, garden, or hair you re-designed for them or even an insight into your own day in the life of.

- Extend this content on an Instagram post, using carousels to share more context and details.
- Tweak the language in your stories and re-use on LinkedIn.
- Take the context to create some bite-sized magic, like X (Twitter) threads or TikTok tales.
- Extend your stories with more context and add emotionally driven content for podcasting episodes and blogs; perfect for building a loyal following or engaged community.

And, if all else fails and your mind is just not going to play ball, cut yourself a break. Go and do something else. Get a change of scenery. Pick up your laptop or notebook and head out of the office. Cafe's work a treat for me, plus there's always the benefit of added cake.

USING CUSTOMER STORIES TO BUILD TRUST AND CREDIBILITY

A terrible tale of what happens when you tell one story but deliver another

Chatting with a friend over a beer, we quickly established that we used the same supplier. And, more interestingly, had both switched our business to them on the promise of a very different type of service that appealed to our own sense of values and purpose. Talk, however, soon turned to mutual feelings of being let down by them. The story we had been sold was a long way from the actual experience working with them and things just weren't adding up. We bitched and moaned about them for a while. Not exactly what the brand would have hoped for two of their separate customers to be doing, I would imagine.

Now I'm not here to slag anyone off and I certainly won't be naming the supplier, no matter how much chocolate you try and bribe me with. But I wanted to share this story with you to show you what happens when you say one thing and act another.

As we've discussed at length, the reason storytelling in business is so powerful is because it creates deep emotional connections with your audience, building trust and respect. However, that trust and respect can be quickly broken if the experience your customers get working with you or buying from you is a long way from your story. The classic case of fur coat no knickers.

How do you make sure your story is consistent with reality so you can benefit from all the great things that trust can bring you as a business?

Here are my top tips:

1. Make sure everything you talk about – your purpose, your vision, your values aligns to what you truly believe, not just what you think others want to hear, or what you feel you need to say to differentiate yourself.

2. Be prepared to evidence everything – either with examples of how you work, customer stories or, when

it comes to values, be able to show how you live and breathe them every day.

3. If things change – maybe your business grows really quickly, you take on a bigger team or even shift direction, make sure you update your story. Your customer's will understand. If you lie to them, they won't.

4. Make sure you are always thinking about your audience and who you want to attract. Read. The. Room. For example boasting about hitting large targets when you've just hiked up your prices may leave a sour taste...

5. Be consistent. You never know when two of your customers might be sipping on an ice cold beverage talking about you...

Customer Success Stories are Ready-made Content. So why are we so scared to share them?

- It feels awkward – like I'm bragging. Does anyone really want to see this stuff?
- I've shared testimonials and I got low engagement – I don't think my audience likes this type of content.
- I ask my customers for a testimonial or review and they're really boring.
- My customer doesn't want me to share that I'm working with them.

- I ask my customers but they're always so busy and never get round to writing me a review.
- Everything I write sounds really dull and doesn't reflect my other content, so I don't want to share it.

Imagine being able to unblock whatever is holding you back from sharing your customer success stories? Wouldn't it feel good to be able to talk about all your great work without feeling the ick or worrying that people think you're boasting? And in doing so have ready-made powerful content on tap?

If the idea of sharing case studies, testimonials and success story fills you with dread, even though you know you probably – no definitely – should be doing more of it. Or if asking your customers for a review brings on a hot sweat even though you know they're really happy with what you've helped them with. Rest assured, you're not alone.

Linked to Imposter Syndrome, a natural modesty that's engrained in us, or fear of judgement or being seen as a bit boastful (thanks society for making us women feel THAT one), it's a really common occurrence with most of the business owners I work with.

As a result, we never get to hear about the impact you're making or, worse still, the world gets another dull case study that doesn't really tell us anything (sorry if that's you – but I can help you make them more meaningful).

I believe that it all starts with mindset. Rather than thinking about all the horrible, yucky things that you normally associate with asking for and sharing testimonials, let's consider what happens when you share a positive customer experience.

- It's READY MADE STORY CONTENT (have I mentioned that already?) that's perfect for re-purposing across all your different platforms and marketing activities including social media posts, blogs, your website, YouTube, awards entries, webinars or newsletters.

- You're providing invaluable credibility about the value you offer to others – that's unbeatable even by the very best sales copy or fanciest website.

- Sharing testimonials reinforces your relationship with your customer, helping build loyalty and making it more likely they will tell others about you (that illusive W.O.M – word of mouth that we're all seeking).

- Reading stories of how others have succeeded as a result of working with you or using your products, actually reduces the fear factor for potential customers wondering whether or not to invest in you. Being able to see and FEEL how others have been impacted by what you do gives them confidence in their decision making and can sometimes be the thing that finally pushes them over the fence to buy from you (all that good logical reasoning to reinforce their emotional gut feel … remember?!)

Bottom line. Sharing your successes doesn't make you look like a prize numpty. But ignoring the opportunity for ready-made content that is really going to connect to the needs of your audience and that you can use time and time again, does.

And, as an added bonus, as well as great content, testimonials provide insight and inform your marketing and business model. Winner, winner, chicken dinner!

There are two ways in which you can create customer success content. Firstly – you can ask for a testimonial (yes, I know it's scary but we've already talked about this…). Without almost any extra work, you can turn what your customer shares with you into at the very least an Instagram post or a quote for your website. But, if you ask the right questions, you can take their content and turn it into something a little more powerful – a customer success story.

But first things first, and I'm sure plenty of you will identify with this. How do you stop your customer from sending you a dull review?

You know what I'm talking about. You wait patiently for weeks for that all illusive review. You know your customer is ecstatic about what you've done for them. And then they send you this:

"I loved working with Hilary, she really helped my business. I would highly recommend her."

GAHHHHHHHH!!

You've got three options. You can post it like it is, knowing it serves next to no value to anyone. You can re-write it yourself (cheeky I know). Or, and it will be no surprise this is my preferred route, you can be more specific with them to start with to make sure you get the content you need from them.

It's all about asking the right questions, digging a little deeper and giving your customers just a gentle steering hand (questionnaires or online surveys are great for this) and before you know it, you'll be getting share-worthy testimonials just like this:

"I came to Hilary because I'd reached a brick wall with my coaching biz. My web copy was stopping me attracting new customers and I was struggling to grow.

Hilary put me at ease straight away and it was clear she 'just got me.'

I now have a brilliantly written website and sales conversion numbers are up. And I have someone I trust to help me again in the future."

My Secret Sauce Questions for Great Customer Testimonials:

What inspired you to buy from me?

- What was life like before buying from me?
- What did you need to change?

What was your biggest challenge?

- How did it impact you day to day?
- What did you fear the most?

What helped you make the decision to buy from me?

• What did you hope you would be able to do that you haven't been able to do before?

What did you enjoy most about working with me/using my product?

• How would you describe the experience?

How specifically did I or my product help you?

• How has this impacted your life?
• What do you think/feel/do differently now?

What would you tell someone else who is experiencing the same as you were?

Writing Your First Customer Story

Putting your customer at the heart of your stories will show potential clients just how you can improve their lives with the products or services you provide. It also provides a unique twist on the rather tiresome – 'Challenge, Solution, Benefit' case study that we all know and (don't actually) love.

Once you have a testimonial – or even if you haven't, you can start to write your first customer success story that you can use on your website, your social media, your presentations and your pitches.

FOLLOW THE FRAMEWORK BELOW TO START
PLOTTING OUT YOUR STORY.

Who is your main character?

Who are they, what do they do?

What problem were they trying to solve and why?

What did they need to achieve?

Why did they really need what you sell? What was standing in their way?

Look beyond the obvious things you fixed and think about their fears. Why did they really need what you sell? Use your customer's words here to make the story more powerful.

What happened when they met you or bought your products or services?

How did they find you? What was the experience like for them? How did they know you were the right person to help them?

How did you work together to solve their problem or how did your product/service solve their problem?

What plan / reassurances did you give them? How did the relationship between you and them help this? How did you motivate and support them? Did you give them a how-to guide?

How might things have gone had they not found you, your products or services?

This could be something tangible like missing out on a sale for a business owner or a feeling, like remaining unfulfilled or frustrated.

What did you help them avoid?

Like wasting time worrying, investing in the wrong solution, being fearful of change etc.

How did things improve for them in the end? What did success look and feel like for them?

How did things get better for them? What are they able to do now that they couldn't before and how does this make them feel?

What has this taught you?

What learnings can you take from this which will help you support other similar customers in the future? What does this mean for your ideal client reading this story?

What do you want your audience to do as a result of reading this story?

If someone wants to experience similar to the character in your story, what do they have to do next and how do they do it? This is your call-to-action.

Finally – you need a summary to go at the top of your story to draw people in, but I always recommend leaving this bit to last. Once you've answered all the questions above, try summarising the story in 1-2 lines with the successful outcome as the perfect hook. Here is an example for a customer story I created for a land developer.

Headline: *Solving a complex planning puzzle to honour a family man's last wishes and generate a high return.*

Body copy: *With perseverance and a healthy dose of creativity, we turned derelict scrubland into a valuable asset generating a regular monthly income for our client and creating an exciting project for us. Read on to find out how we did it.*

A brilliant customer success story should leave your customers with four key questions they simply have to come to you to answer:

Question 1: "What do I have to do to feel like that too?"

Use emotion to show, not just what happened to your customer, but how it made them feel.

Question 2: "How could my life change too?"

Include loads of juicy details on how you made your customers' lives easier, more joyful, etc and what you enabled them to do next.

Question 3: "I'm experiencing exactly the same – could this work for me too?"

Don't just share the result, but the reason your customer bought from you in the first place. What problem were they trying to solve, why hadn't they been able to solve it before, and how was it making them feel?

Question 4: "I'm ready to feel like that customers does. Where do I sign up?"

Make sure you've got a super clear call to action. This could be a Calendly link to book a call with you, a sign up form or a buy-now button.

Work in Practice:

Making People the Story for Global Events Business, Evolve Events

All too often when we write about the work we do, we focus on the functional. In the case of Evolve Events who have pulled off some of the most spectacular celebratory events I've ever seen, their stories typically looked at how they had transformed a certain space to fit the brief of their client. Interesting? Maybe. Different from their competition? Most definitely not. And the founders Anna and Gary Peters recognised this, calling me in to help.

I took a 'We transformed an empty space to something beautiful for a charity' message and turned it on its head, focussing the message instead on the human impact of the event – 'Charity raised life-changing amount of money to help children at a gala we organised.'

Here is the story in full to give you some inspiration on how to find an interesting angle that will stand your customer success stories apart from your competition:

Ubuntu Success Story

Raising Life-changing Amounts of Funding for South African Children

"The expert advice, passion, commitment, friendship and pure professionalism I received is what I've been looking for, for a very long time." Ubuntu – charity fundraiser

Why? Ubuntu Educational Fund has one all-en-compassing yet radical mission; to change the lives of orphaned and vulnerable children in Port Elizabeth, South Africa, giving them what all children deserve – dignity. They're unable to do this without substantial, long-term funding.

What? Events are a vital part of the charity's fundraising campaigns, raising awareness of the critical work they do and motivating high profile, wealthy guests to pledge their financial support. An empathetic interpretation of the brief was essential to reflect the passion and dedication of the charity.

They needed to work with a team experienced in hosting charity galas and who could work seamlessly with the organising committee and the operational team in SA to bring the charity to life authentically throughout the event.

How? Ubuntu Educational Fund raised a staggering amount of money on the night with BBC Auctioneer Charlie Ross running a live pledge for the 400 guests. More importantly, they secured multi-year commitments for funding their U.ME.WE campaign.

The event left a lasting impression on attendees, surprised by the unusual venue choice (The Old Sorting Office, a raw space in central London, transformed into something beautiful with 'industrial elegance') and clever use of experiences revealed throughout the evening. Like a classroom with sound bites of children laughing. And a cloakroom with name pegs of some of the many children the charity has helped.

As a fitting tribute to Ubuntu Educational Fund's vision that we creatively and sympathetically brought to life, the gala was recognised by the events industry, winning the award for Best Celebration Event.

Using Customer Stories to Help You Sell

Used correctly, customer success stories can do more than just help you build trusted relationships, they can drive customers through the buying cycle and get them to finally part with their cash.

What do I mean by the buying cycle?

OK, time for a bit of marketing theory here that I picked up in my years working for corporate marketing teams. All customers go through a bit of a journey when it comes to buying products or services. Sometimes the journey can be nano-seconds short (imagine seeing a new brand pop up on Facebook selling something you really like the look of, clicking the button and it arriving outside your house the next day) or it can be days, weeks or even months. If you sell high ticket items like consultancy for example, or annual membership communities, your customer may need a bit more time to learn about what you do and assess their options before finally committing.

The clever bods at Smart Insights, an organisation dedicated to helping improve people's digital marketing skills devised a model for this, snappily called RACE – Reach, Act, Convert and Engage. Before you start panicking that this is another thing to learn, fret not. One, it's fairly logical so you're probably already thinking in this way and two, it's just a nice way to break down the type of content you need to produce for your business – a handy way to plan shall we say, rather than a must-do.

REACH

Objective: Grow your audience

- Share lots of social content that grabs attention, raises awareness of your brand and positions you as an expert.
- Share stories that speak directly to your customer's problems to show you understand them.
- Personal experience stories are great here.

ACT

Objective: Prompt interactions, subscribers and leads

- Nurture and educate your customer with your stories.
- Share practical guidance to show your willingness to help – top tips, product videos etc, and build trust.
- Customer success stories work well here but keep them light!

CONVERT

Objective: Get that sale!

- Now's the time to wow!
- You're in the running but your customer needs final persuasion or reassurance.
- Take them through a success story, share a video testimonial, invite them to speak to one of your happy customers.

ENGAGE

Objective: Encourage repeat business and WOM (the holy grail of small biz marketing... word of mouth)

- Promote your customers' content about you through your channels.
- Invite them to share their story and incentivise them.
- Create a platform/community to share experiences with other customers.

CONNECTING IN THE DIGITAL AGE

Tap into the stories your customers are sharing about you

Giving your customers a platform to tell stories about your business is a fantastic way to foster engagement, build trust, and create a sense of community and in the digital era – it's actually something that's easier to do than you think.

Here are some steps you can take to provide your customers with a platform for sharing their stories:

1. **Create a dedicated space:** Set up a dedicated section on your website or create a separate webpage where your customers can share their stories. Make it easily accessible and prominently displayed so it's super easy to find.

2. **Make the most of social media:** Use different social media platforms to create opportunities for your customers to share their experiences and stories. Encourage customers to use a specific hashtag related

to your brand. British womenswear brand Lucy and Yak are brilliant at doing this.

3. **Offer incentives:** Motivate your customers by providing incentives. It could be discounts, exclusive access to new products or services, or even featuring their stories on your website or social media channels. Incentives can help encourage participation and make your customers feel appreciated.

4. **Implement reviews and testimonials:** Incorporate a review or testimonial section on your website where your customers can provide feedback and share their experiences. Google is also good for this. Displaying positive reviews and testimonials from satisfied customers can serve as powerful social proof, building trust and encouraging others to share their stories as well.

5. **Conduct interviews or case studies:** Reach out to your loyal customers and ask if they would be willing to participate in an interview or a case study. This allows you to dive deeper into their experiences with your business, highlighting specific details and outcomes. These stories can be published on your website, blog, or even shared through newsletters.

6. **Host events or webinars:** Invite customers to discuss how your products or services have impacted their lives or businesses at an event – online or IRL. This interactive platform allows for live storytelling and provides a great opportunity for your ideal clients to connect with your existing customers.

7. **Engage with user-generated content:** Keep an eye out for customers who share content related to your brand on their social media. Engage with their posts, repost their content, and show your appreciation for their support. This encourages more customers to share their stories, knowing that they will be acknowledged and celebrated.

Remember to always seek permission from your customers before sharing their stories publicly and respect their privacy. Provide clear guidelines and instructions on how they can share their stories and ensure their consent is obtained.

By providing your customers with a platform to share their stories, you not only give them a voice but also create a community of happy advocates who really care about your business. Their stories will inspire others, build credibility, and strengthen the bond between your brand and your ideal clients.

Use Your Story to Build a Community of Like-minded People, United Behind Your Cause

Let me introduce you to Nature Nurture, a social enterprise based in the UK who are doing things a little differently. Founded by one of the most interesting women I've had the pleasure of working with, Natalie Ganpatsingh, Nature Nurture is not about chasing profits.

Natalie and her team's primary goal is to make a genuine difference in the world, enhancing the mental and physical wellbeing of those living in urban areas by connecting them with the nature on their doorstep – the true definition of a purpose-led organisation. And what's incredible, is that they're doing it, day in day out, creating huge tangible impact on people and the planet but when I first met Natalie, she was struggling to know how best to talk about what they do. Now I know I'm biased, but the answer to me was clear – with such a human angle to everything she does, it could only ever be storytelling. Easier said than done however, especially with so many less virtuous organisations trying to greenwash their customers and making consumers potentially cynical.

Over the last few years, I've seen a growing trend among small independent brands, even those who set up initially with profit in mind, to embrace a more community-oriented and environmentally conscious sense of purpose. It's a powerful acknowledgement that we all have a role to play in shaping the world around us, for better or worse. But how do you tell your story, when you're more about the collective benefit of what you do, rather than the individual. And how can you use that story to attract and unite people being your cause?

I'll share how I helped Nature Nurture with their story-telling, but for now, let's start at the very beginning…

Share the core reason why your business exists and what its purpose is: Let your audience feel the passion that drives you, the values that guide you, and the bigger societal need you're addressing. Let's make it crystal clear why your business is here to make a difference.

Showcase the journey: Every purpose-led story has an incredible journey, and yours is no different. Take your audience on an adventure through the evolution of your purpose-led business. Share the tale of how it all started, the obstacles you faced (and conquered, of course), and the milestones you achieved along the way. Highlight the pivotal moments that shaped your purpose and demonstrate the progress you've made. It's time to sprinkle some fairy dust on your business's story

Share the personal narratives that inspired you to embark on this purpose-led adventure: What experiences, motivations, or anecdotes fuelled your passion? Don't forget to weave in the stories of the individuals your business has touched, be it customers, employees, or community members. These personal touches will bring authenticity and depth to your narrative.

Be honest about your journey, including the challenges you've faced and the lessons you've learned along the way to unlock trust and increase credibility: Avoid the temptation to exaggerate or 'greenwash' your impact. Authenticity is the golden thread that weaves your purpose-led story together.

Make sure you showcase the incredible impact your purpose-led business has made. For Nature Nurture, I created a series of heart-warming stories to illustrate the positive difference they'd made in people's lives and the community. Use tangible evidence to show how your purpose transforms lives and creates meaningful outcomes. Craft narratives that resonate deeply with your target audience, leaving them spellbound by your mission.

Here's an example of a story I created for Nature Nurture:

> ## Holy Brook Nook – The flag-ship community regeneration venture that's left a sizeable legacy
>
> *How utilising Reading Borough Council's Community Infrastructure Levy opened a world of opportunity for the people of Coley and the wider environment.*
>
> We still have to pinch ourselves when we think about how much we achieved at Holy Brook Nook, a run-down area of Reading that had previously been known for crime and persistent drug use.
>
> Conservation, a play and learning space, public art, walking programmes, community events and a community garden, the list is substantial. We've strengthened our existing partnerships and forged new ones. And have successfully engaged local schools and the community to co-create a thriving natural community and outdoor learning space that everyone feels proud of and are keen to protect.
>
> But the project hasn't been without its challenges; clearing hazardous rubbish, managing homeless people and drug use on site, anti-social behaviour and even a fire. Our commitment to making a change, and the will of all those involved from the

groups we collaborated with to the local residents and schools, drove us to keep going, no matter what.

Co-creation ensures community is at the heart of our projects

Our first point of call was to meet with those living close by. Our facilitated community engagement events, enabled us, and our partners, to understand the challenges and fears residents had about Holy Brook Book, listen to what ideas they had for regeneration and encouraged them to get involved.

Wanting to make sure all our activities were therapeutic and supportive, we ensured everyone felt welcome, regardless of their abilities or gardening experience and continue to provide a range of nature-based interventions and events to suit all.

For so many people living in Coley who'd spent their lives avoiding Holy Brook Nook, the transformation was something quite incredible:

"My first time helping with work at the Holy Brook Nook site was the first thing that I'd done since Covid lockdowns that wasn't specifically for people with mental health issues. It's opened my horizons! I don't know yet where it will take me next, but I now feel there's a positive world out there – in nature and in people and in further travels. In the meantime, I know

I have a welcome, positive work, good company and so much new to learn, at Holy Brook Nook." Jane

Remember, your purpose-led story is what connects all aspects of your business. Ensure that your story remains consistent across all touch-points and interactions with your audience. From your marketing materials to your website content, social media presence, and customer communications, let your purpose shine through.

REFLECT AND REIMAGINE

Everything you do from this point onwards is a work-in-progress. There is no fixed end point with storytelling, no gold medal to collect after a marathon well run. Storytelling is a way of life, of business that will ebb and flow with you as you grow, learn and develop.

- Take the time, as you to listen to feedback, tap into your audience and seek more feedback, to understand the impact of your stories and how you need to adjust them along the way.

- If something doesn't land as you would have expected, rather than reject it altogether (or more likely beat yourself up), take the time to understand why people didn't engage with it as much as other content and use these reflections to refine and enhance your approach as a storyteller. Lean into your audience, ask them questions, run polls and surveys and acknowledge their responses.

And don't forget how far you've come. Take the time every now and again to reflect on what you've learned and celebrate the wins, big and small, along the way. Better still, share these reflections with your audience to make them feel like they're sitting in the passenger seat alongside you, not outside staring in.

Let's Address the Elephant in the Room – Time

I'll cut to the chase, you've come a long way and you're almost at the end of this book. You've faced up to your fears, you feel more confident about who you are and what your voice can do, you've got a heap of ideas for stories you could be telling but there's still one problem which unfortunately even I can't fix. Time. Or rather a lack of it.

Running a business means wearing multiple hats some of which fit perfectly for you, others which make you look like your great Aunt Annie. Or in other words, you can't be brilliant at everything nor can you invent extra hours in the day to fit in doing what you do brilliantly, running a business, marketing a business, having a life, sleeping, eating. The concept of 'the woman who has it all' is bullshit. No woman in their right mind would really want it all. And that, thankfully, is where outsourcing comes in.

Firstly there is a massive caveat to what I am about to say. You really need to outsource to someone who knows what they're doing. Hiring the wrong person, without a track record in business storytelling, no matter how brilliant they are at writing, is a false economy and can leave you with a massive heartache and an empty purse.

On the other hand, working closely with someone who has the tools and experience to take on your story as if it were their own, in your voice and style, can free you up to focus on just wearing that hat that really suits you.

If you're unsure whether you need to invest in outside help in your business (storytelling or otherwise), here are a few questions to consider.

Firstly, what would it cost you to do XYZ task yourself? Your immediate thought might be, "Well nothing, it's just me." So break it down.

What would it cost you in time? And what would it take you away from doing?

Imagine writing your brand story and turning it into web copy for the launch of your new website. Think about all the other things you could be doing with that time, like selling or delivering client work. If you paid someone, say £1500 to do the job for you, how much could you charge your own clients in that time? Or how many units of product could you sell to recoup the cost?

What about the cost to your sanity?

The stress of doing something that isn't your core strength and isn't the reason you got into business may actually prevent you ever launching that new product, pressing 'go-live' on your website or starting that community group you feel so passionate about. And what a great shame that would be eh?

Outsourcing may feel like a luxury you can't afford right now but before you dismiss it outright, really think about the lost opportunity cost of not doing it.

There is no right or wrong answer to the question of outsourcing storytelling and copywriting but I am certain of one thing – you are not a fictional super hero. You cannot be brilliant at everything, all of the time and there is definitely no weakness in asking for help. In fact, it can be such a smart business move, it's quite the opposite.

THE GOOD STUFF TO REMEMBER

Being a good business storyteller isn't about showcasing grand successes but rather about finding the unique and insightful angles that make you stand out from the crowd and resonate with your audience. Stories are everywhere, from your personal experiences to community impact and they go a long way to humanise your brand so you can connect with your dream clients on a person-to-person basis – rather than being a faceless organisation.

Customer trust and credibility are built upon the alignment between the stories you tell about your business and the actual experiences your clients have. Consistency between your narrative and reality is crucial for maintaining trust and a positive brand reputation. Sharing the success stories of your clients not only validates your brand's promises but is also invaluable content; ready-made stories you can share across your marketing channels to inspire, engage and convert your dream clients.

By providing platforms for customers to share their experiences, offering incentives and engaging with user-generated content, you can broaden your reach, create impactful social proof and build a loyal client base.

GET READY TO ROAR

So you're ready to tell your first business story? Woah, Nelly, not so fast. I love your storytelling enthusiasm but before you press send, let's check the basics.

- Have you defined your ideal customer?
- Does your story talk directly to them and the problem they are trying to solve?
- Does your headline or first sentence create enough appeal and intrigue to grab someone's attention?
- Is it obvious what you're talking about and why they should care?
- Is it clear how you can help and how this would solve their specific problem?
- Does it answer the 'so-what test'? Are the benefits to your customer crystal clear?
- Does the language and tone match your audience? Is it too formal or too chatty?

- Have you included enough sensory details to trigger a more emotional response, for example, sounds, feelings, tastes, etc?

- Have you cut any waffle, fluff, or unnecessary words (including those that you would never use in person)?

- Have you used contractions to make your writing sound more human and less wordy, eg, using 'you'll' instead of you will or 'would've' instead of would have?

- Have you used real-life or made-up examples to bring your stories to life and make them easier to understand and relate to?

- Would your granny or an alien landing on earth understand what you're talking about and why it's important?

- Is there a clear call to action so customers know what you want them to do next?

CHAPTER 7
ROAR

"Women challenge the status quo because we're never it."

Cindy Gallop

UNDERSTANDING YOUR ROLE: THE RESPONSIBILITY OF WOMEN AS STORYTELLERS

Having a voice is not just about winning over your audience or connecting with your dream clients. It's about what that voice can do.

There's no question that I was treated differently in my early career from my male peers. Paid less, passed over for promotion (when I knew I was the more skilled, let down by my own modesty), sexualised, hit on by creepy old men, including my boss and a very strange chap from IT just because they thought they could get away with it. But it wasn't until I started opening up about my experiences with others and, more importantly realising that I was far from alone, did I realise the true impact of phrases that have sadly become all too commonplace in our everyday speech; gender bias, pay gap, inequality, discrimination, bullying, sexual assault. But by the same force in which I had my eyes opened to just how many women experience this, I also learned something else – the power of stories to take the fucking awful and transform it into a massive rolling engine for change. And why?

Because stories make our world bigger.

Storytelling shapes our understanding, connects us to one another and inspires change. Stories give us a route to get to know people we may never meet and take us on a journey inside their lives, so we see what they see and feel what they feel, opening our eyes to the good and bad and teaching us to be better humans.

As women, we have a unique responsibility to embrace our role as storytellers and explore the transformative power of our narratives to challenge societal norms, create a more inclusive business landscape and redefine what it means to identify as female today.

Our stories can break through the confines of traditional gender roles and inspire others to pursue their dreams fearlessly. By sharing our experiences, triumphs, and challenges, we provide hope and pave the way for future generations of women to re-write the stories that have stood in our way for decades.

Women, and those that identify as female, encompass a rich tapestry of experiences, background and perspectives. As storytellers, we can amplify these diverse voices, celebrate differences and provide space for a wide range of narratives to be heard. By sharing stories from different cultures, ethnicities, abilities and social backgrounds we contribute to a more inclusive and empathetic society, creating spaces for dialogue, understanding, and collaboration. Our narratives can ignite conversations around important topics such as gender equality, social justice, mental health, and more. Through our storytelling, we can catalyse change and rally others to join us in creating a more equitable and compassionate world.

Providing Hope for Others

Our stories have the power to empower and inspire. When we embrace our own struggles and share how we've triumphed over them, we give others the courage to embrace their own paths and overcome obstacles. In a word, we give them hope.

Our narratives can shed light on issues that are often overlooked or silenced, sparking conversations and driving positive change. When we share our vulnerabilities and successes, we create a supportive community where women can find strength, inspiration, and the belief that they, too, can make a difference.

As women, we carry the stories of those who came before us. It is our responsibility to preserve and honour the struggles, triumphs, and contributions of women throughout history. By sharing these stories, we ensure that their legacies continue to inspire and guide us. We celebrate their achievements, amplify their voices, and pave the way for future generations to continue the journey towards equality.

Using Your Story to Address and Overcome Prejudice

I know that words don't replace action, and the right for equality needs to be more than something we just tell stories about, but our words do matter and they do hold weight when used effectively. Using your personal story and providing a platform for others to do the same, can be a powerful way to challenge biases.

Own your narrative:
Take ownership of your story and embrace it with confidence. By sharing your personal experiences, you provide a human face to counter stereotypes and challenge prejudiced assumptions. Be proud of your unique background, heritage, or identity, and use your story as a tool for education and enlightenment.

Educate and inform:
Prejudice often stems from ignorance and lack of understanding. Use your story as a platform for education and awareness. Share insights into your experiences, culture, or perspective to help others gain a deeper understanding of your background and challenge any misconceptions they may have.

Engage in dialogue:

Open up channels for dialogue and conversation. Create opportunities for honest and respectful discussions where people can ask questions and learn from one another. By engaging in meaningful conversations, you can address prejudices directly, clarify misunderstandings, and promote empathy and understanding.

Share personal impact:

Highlight the positive impact that diversity and inclusion have had on your life and the lives of others. Illustrate how embracing different perspectives and experiences enriches communities and organisations. By sharing stories of collaboration, teamwork, and innovation that arise from diverse environments, you can counter prejudice by demonstrating the value of inclusion.

Connect on a human level:

Focus on the shared human experiences that transcend prejudice. Share stories that highlight universal themes of love, compassion, resilience, and hope. By emphasising our common humanity, you can bridge divides and foster empathy, helping others see beyond prejudice and connect with you on a deeper level.

Be authentic and vulnerable:

Authenticity and vulnerability are powerful tools to challenge prejudice. Share your personal struggles, challenges, and triumphs. By exposing your vulnerabilities, you create an environment where others can relate and empathise with your experiences, dismantling preconceived notions and fostering compassion.

Advocate for change:

Use your story as a catalyst for change. Advocate for policies, practices, and initiatives that promote equality, diversity, and inclusion. Participate in community events, organisations, or movements that work towards eradicating prejudice. By taking action, you not only empower yourself but also inspire others to confront their biases and work towards a more inclusive society.

Build a strong network or community around you:

Remember, changing deeply ingrained prejudice takes time and effort. Your story is a powerful tool, but it may not change everyone's perspective immediately. Focus on planting seeds of understanding, one person at a time, and trust in the power of storytelling to gradually break down barriers and create a more inclusive world.

> How one woman's personal story became a beacon of hope for other neurodiverse people
>
> Meet Laura Neville. Laura is an entrepreneur and founder of adaptogenic wellness brand, The Herbtender. She's an ADHD advocate and loves rhinos (trust me, that's an important detail).
>
> When I met Laura, she'd recently been diagnosed with ADHD. We discussed the challenges of combining her brand purpose and story with her

personal experiences. Understandably she was worried that people might judge (misjudge?) her and was worried about diluting her brand message – she co-founded The Herbtender with her husband Mark, so the story is not exclusively hers, a common challenge when you're not a company of one.

However, unpicking her personal story, it soon became clear how closely everything was linked. Laura has struggled for years with insomnia. In her pursuit of a better night's sleep, she had stumbled upon adaptogens – natural substances like herbs, plants and mushrooms that help the body cope with stress and regain balance – perfect for sleep and more. Excited by the opportunities this presented, Laura and Mark, supported by in-house medical herbalist Schia Sinclair, founded The Herbtender.

A year after launching the business, fate had an unexpected revelation in store for Laura. She received some life-altering news – she was diagnosed with ADHD. As she and her family slowly adapted to this new found reality, she embarked on a profound journey of self-discovery, determined to reframe her understanding of who she was. And, along with Schia sought ways to manage her ADHD and enhance her quality of life. Through their relentless dedication, they discovered the power of supplements like their Calm & Collected formulation, tailor-made for individuals like Laura, who often feel too wired to be productive or need help to calm down before bedtime.

Now, Laura's mission lies in helping others – especially those living with neurodiverse conditions like ADHD – embrace the potential of adaptogens for a healthier, calmer and focussed life. And that's the story she tells with confidence. That and how every month a portion of The Herbtender's profits go to a rhino-centric conservation charity in South Africa; another example of Laura's personal values and her desire to contribute positively to the people and word around her – all part of a compelling story that seeks to educate, inform and advocate for change.

In the words of Laura, "It felt like I had a huge mountain to climb, but now I'm clear on who I am and the difference my experiences can make to others going through similar, it's so much easier to share my story and know how to link it with our brand story as well."

My Personal Responsibility

"Be the role model you never had."

These words resonate hard with me. Up until I went to secondary school, my mum didn't have a paid job. I say it that way because of course she had a job; she had three children to look after and a house to run whilst my GP father went to work. All my friends' mums were in the same situation. No-one I knew ran their own business. The only woman I looked up to was BBC war reporter Kate Adie. I thought she was über cool and hard as nails but, despite wanting to be a journalist myself, I never once thought her role would be one I could consider. And quite frankly, I'm glad I didn't – but you get my point. Growing up in the 70s, 80s or even 90s, successful women running their own business was the exception not the norm. At school we read novels written by men. We learnt about history involving mainly white men and one lesson on the Suffragettes. Our careers talks focused solely on caring roles; nurses, teachers; all very important roles but never once we were told as girls that we could aspire to anything else. And this is bollocks. I've had to learn the hard way that if you want something enough, you can get it but you'll come up against barrier after barrier along the way, not least to do with the fact you have a vagina rather than a penis.

Now, as a mother to a teenage daughter, I'm hugely conscious of the impact I have on her – good and bad and the responsibility that this brings. Both myself and her stepfather Tim run our own businesses – so that's a start. She gets to enjoy the rewards of that; the flexibility it provides to watch her dance performances, pick her up when she's feeling poorly, always having someone at home when she gets in from school, the nice holidays when we've had a good year. But she also sees the hard side of it; the inconsistent wages, the long hours, the self-doubt, the questioning. She gets to see the struggle that both of us face from time to time with our own worth, the judgements made on us and the impact of criticism and failure. But also the successes. Neither myself or Tim hide the realities of working for ourselves – we make sure to celebrate the wins with her and breakdown the difficulties over eggs, bacon and beans during lazy weekend brunches.

At the very least, I hope she'll see the thing that I didn't at her age – that she has options. In fact, she has a whole world of choices, paths to take, places to go, things to learn that will not be restricted by preconceived ideas of what her limits are based purely on her gender. I can't say whether or not she'll own her own business in the future but she will know it's possible, if it's the right thing for her, and hopefully she'll spread the word to her friends too.

Because, when young girls see successful women sharing their business stories - and by successful I don't just mean those that earn big bucks and flash it around on Insta, real women achieving their own mark of happiness and success, it ignites a spark within them. It gives them role models to look up to and motivates them to pursue their dreams fearlessly. By showcasing the achievements, challenges, and triumphs of female entrepreneurs and business leaders, we empower the next generation of women to believe in themselves and pursue their own aspirations, whatever they are. But also to do it in a way that values and rewards their confidence and commitment to continuing positive change in the way they've seen others do before them.

WHAT DOES IT REALLY MEAN TO ROAR?

At the start of this book, I made you a promise. Not that I would give you all the answers, because honestly, that's just not how life works, but instead, to arm you with the know-how, the tools, the skills to take your story into the world with the confidence that not only people are going to listen to what you have to say but that it's going to make a difference. To them, to you and your business and to the world, the future generation of female business owners and leaders.

Being able to Roar is not about being the best, the loudest, the most polished, the richest, the skinniest, the cleverest. It's about accepting your story is enough because it's **your** story, not someone else's narrative or view of success. And it's about sharing your story in a way that feels like you, connecting you to the people that matter in a genuine way that uplifts you, brings you strength at your darkest times and creates positive change – loudly or quietly.

To Roar is to be unafraid to share your stories or, when that's not possible, to be strong enough to face your fears and do it anyway. Remember, this stuff "isn't hard because you're doing it wrong. It's hard because it's hard." (Thanks Lauren Currie, OBE, for that quote – I live and die by it)

When you Roar, and you do it truthfully, passionately, selflessly, you will find comfort in knowing your story – no matter how tough it is to tell – can and will help others (but only if you share it). You call to others to Roar with you, not to dictate or force opinions but because you know that when we come together, we get stronger, in ourselves and as a group. And it's that strength, the power of combined voices, that can impact the change we need, as women, as business owners, as leaders, to be recognised and rewarded for our confidence, our expertise and our lived experiences, not have them used against us.

So How Do You Do This?

A long time ago, I promised myself never to stand in the shadows again. And I would love for you to make the same commitment to yourself.

As I've said, this book was always going to be more than words on a page. It's a call for action to rise up and use our voices and tell our stories because we know when we do this, it helps other women to do the same.

That's why I've created **The Storytelling Manifesto for Women Who Roar**

You can go online to www.theroarofherstory.com to print off your own copy to sign. Whether you choose to share this publicly is your choice alone but I know from my own experiences that committing openly to those around me that support and care for me, helps hold me accountable for the things I feel most strongly about. If it's the same for you, you can also download sticker gifs to share on your social media and a pledge logo to add to your website.

THE STORYTELLING MANIFESTO
FOR WOMEN WHO ROAR

We, women in business, recognise the power of our unique stories in shaping our future, inspiring others, and creating a positive impact. By using our voice and sharing our experiences, we create connections, provide hope and inspiration and lead with authenticity and courage so other women can lead too.

Our Commitment to Storytelling

1. Being true to ourselves

•   I pledge to share my story with honesty and transparency, embracing both the good times and the bad.

•   I will honour my true self in every story, ensuring my voice remains genuine and unaltered.

2. Backing others

•   I commit to using my story to uplift and inspire other women, creating a supportive community that does not judge.

•   I will highlight the strengths and achievements of others, alongside my own, recognising the collective power of shared experiences.

3. Being courageous

• I vow to not let fear and self-doubt get in my way, boldly sharing my story even when it makes me feel vulnerable.

• I will stand firm in the face of criticism, understanding that my story holds value and deserves to be heard.

4. Focussing on connection

• I aim to create meaningful connections through my storytelling, fostering understanding and empathy to drive positive change.

• I will listen actively to the stories of others, valuing their perspectives and experiences and share them with my community to spread these stories far and wide.

5. Always learning

• I pledge to embrace creativity in my storytelling, using diverse formats and platforms to reach and inspire my audience.

• I will remain open to new ideas and methods, continually evolving my narrative approach.

6. Creating impact

- I commit to using my story as a catalyst for positive change, advocating for issues that matter to me and my community.

- I will measure the impact of my storytelling, seeking ways to amplify my message and broaden my reach.

7. Leaving a legacy

- I vow to build a legacy through my storytelling, leaving a lasting impact for future generations of women in business

- I will document and share the evolution of my journey, ensuring my story continues to inspire long after I am gone.

By signing this manifesto, I affirm my dedication to letting my story Roar. I understand that my voice is powerful, my experiences are valuable, and my narrative can make a difference.

Signature:_____

Date:_____

Congratulations on taking the first step towards embracing and sharing your unique journey.

You are joining a community of strong, powerful women in business who believe in the transformative power of storytelling to achieve whatever success looks and feels like for them.

Let's empower each other, inspire change, and let our stories Roar.

With strength and solidarity,

Your friend in storytelling, Hilary Salzman.

ACKNOWLEDGMENTS

To my darling Tim, thanks for giving me the space to explore who I am and never doubting me. You've taught me to dream bigger than I ever thought was possible. Your unconditional support and love mean the world to me.

To Mum and Dad, thank you for letting me lock myself away in your annex and write this book (and for all the tea and cake you kindly provided).

To Alex, for reaffirming, I wasn't indeed crazy to want to write a book, and being patient as I cancelled weekends together to meet my deadline.

To Honor for always being my cheerleader and encouraging Huxley, Rufus and Walter to ROAR!

To Amy, Pam, Belinda, Helen, Penny, Elsie, Roz and Suzi. You ladies rock. You know why.

To Steph, thank you for championing the idea of this book from day one and getting the early manuscript over the line with your encouragement and positive feedback. I also thank Jessica for teaching me how to write a kick-ass book proposal.

To Nicola at The Unbound Press for her magical approach to publishing and dedication to transformative storytelling. I will forever be grateful that the universe introduced us.

And finally, to all the inspiring women I've had the pleasure of helping tell their stories, there would be no book without you. Thank you for believing in me, as I believe in you. This is just the beginning.

Get ready to Roar!

CONTRIBUTORS

A heartfelt thanks to the inspiring people I've had the pleasure of working with who were happy for me to share their stories in this book.

Dr Katie Morris, The Purple House Clinic
www.thepurplehouseclinic.co.uk

Roz Berkeley-Hill and Abi Tippetts, Tipperleyhill
www.tipperleyhill.com

Belinda Knott, Pothies www.pothies.co.uk

Helen Perry www.helen-perry.co.uk

Rebecca Crayford, RCLM www.rebeccacrayford.co.uk

Bobbi Montgomery Heath
www.linkedin.com/in/bobbiheath

Richard Sharman, Gladstn London
www.gladstnlondon.com

Anna Peters, Evolve Events www.evolve-events.com

Natalie Ganpatsingh, Nature Nurture
www.nature-nurture.co.uk

Laura Neville, The Herbtender
www.the-herbtender.co.uk

Nicola O'Byrne www.breastfeedingsupport.ie

ABOUT THE AUTHOR

Hilary Salzman is a business storyteller, writer, podcast host, and speaker, dedicated to helping female business owners who struggle to use their voices and tell their stories confidently.

Hilary brings a unique and refreshing blend of professional storytelling and marketing experience and a personal journey that resonates powerfully with many other women. Having navigated a successful career shift from corporate brand marketing to the marketing agency she founded and, five years later, leaving the 6-figure salary behind to build a storytelling business on her terms, Hilary intimately understands the struggle of being authentic in a world clouded by self-doubt and limiting beliefs.

Hilary's passion for storytelling and commitment to changing the narrative for women over 40, coupled with a strategic knowledge of traditional storytelling techniques and how to incorporate these into your business without feeling the dreaded overwhelm, ensures that *The Roar of Her Story* is not just theoretical but a practical guide that offers a roadmap for female business owners to use real stories to authentically connect with their audience, attract their dream clients and build a business that unapologetically reflects their true selves.

Hilary's podcast, *The Everyday Storyteller*, a daily show for women with something to say, was shortlisted for Business and Self Improvement Podcast of the Year at the Independent Podcast Awards 2023 and 'Moment of Entrepreneurial Inspiration' at the International Women in Podcasting Awards 2023. You can now listen on Spotify, Apple Podcasts, and all major podcast platforms.

Hilary runs personal and business brand workshops and 1:1 training, coaching and mentoring. She is a regular public speaker on various storytelling topics including personal brand storytelling, using storytelling to build an online audience and storytelling for leadership. She is a guest lecturer at Oxford Brookes University, running a seminar on personal branding in the digital era for students studying for a BA in Journalism, Publishing and Media,

Hilary lives in Wiltshire with her partner Tim, daughter Esme, and golden retriever Charlie. This is her first non-fiction book.

HILARY SALZMAN

~

STAY CONNECTED

Access a wide range of business storytelling resources, including the templates mentioned in this book at **www.theroarofherstory.com**

Follow Hilary on social media:

Substack: Speaking In Stories

Instagram @hilarysalzmanstories

TikTok @hilarysalzmanstories

LinkedIn: linkedin.com/in/hilarysalzman/

To book a 1:1 consultancy or brand story workshop, speaking engagement or for any press and media enquiries,
email **hello@hilarysalzman.com**
or visit **www.hilarysalzman.com**

Milton Keynes UK
Ingram Content Group UK Ltd.
UKHW021856231024
450133UK00016B/1013

9 781916 529229